Future
design
for older
people

AGE-FRIENDLY
HOUSING

Future design for older people

AGE-FRIENDLY HOUSING

Julia Park and Jeremy Porteus

RIBA ₩ Publishing

© RIBA Publishing, 2018

Published by RIBA Publishing, 66 Portland Place, London, W1B 1NT

ISBN 9781859468104

9781859468111 (PDF)

British Library Cataloguing-in-Publication Data
A catalogue record for this book is available from the British Library.

Commissioning Editor: Ginny Mills
Project Editors: Daniel Culver /Jane Rogers
Production: Jane Rogers
Designed and Typeset by Mercer Design, London
Printed and bound by Page Bros, Norwich

Cover image: Ørestad Retirement Home, Copenhagen Municipality (Case Study 13)

www.ribapublishing.com

" *Older people face increasing challenges due to the sensory and other changes that age brings. In an age-friendly community, policies, services and structures related to the physical and social environment are designed to support and enable older people to "age actively" – that is, to live in security, enjoy good health and continue to participate fully in society. Public and commercial settings and services are made accessible to accommodate varying levels of ability. Age-friendly service providers, public officials, community leaders, faith leaders and business people:*

- *recognise the great diversity among older persons,*
- *promote their inclusion and contribution in all areas of community life,*
- *respect their decisions and lifestyle choices, and*
- *anticipate and respond flexibly to ageing-related needs and preferences.*

" *An age-friendly community benefits people of all ages. Improving air and water quality protects growing children and older persons with environmental sensitivities. Secure neighbourhoods are safe for children, youth, women and older adults. Families experience less worry and stress when their older relations have the services and supports they need. Barrier-free buildings and streets enhance the mobility and independence of both younger and older persons with disabilities. The whole community benefits from the participation of older persons in volunteer or paid work and civic activities. Finally, the local economy benefits from the patronage of older adult consumers.*

World Health Organization (WHO)[1]

Contents

Foreword

The fact that we are all living longer should be an unequivocal cause for celebration, as more people are able to enjoy a long and fulfilling retirement in which many of the illnesses and occupational hazards that blighted previous generations are no longer to be feared. However, the collective failure to respond to and address the challenges as well as the benefits of ageing means that many people still fear the consequences of growing old. Chief among these is the challenge of housing.

The vast majority of our housing stock is not built with the needs of older people in mind. There are still far too few suitable new homes being delivered, and many older people are living in homes which are unable to meet their changing needs. Housing must be at the centre of our collective conversation about ageing – for far too many people, the decision to move home in later life is precipitated by a crisis in their existing home. This is the case despite strong evidence that those who are able to think proactively about the type of home that will meet their changing needs, and who move before they are too frail to play an active role in their new community, have better outcomes than those who move later.

There is also significant evidence that the vast majority of older people do not want to have to move later in life, which points to the pressing need for design standards to require new homes to be built with much higher levels of accessibility and adaptability. The housing industry is very responsive to policy, and capable of delivering new design standards over time without adding to cost, but it needs leadership from government in order to do so.

Older people are as diverse as people of any age, and our approach to housing must reflect this, providing options for a range of household sizes and types. Design standards matter to older people, both specifically in relation to accessibility and adaptability but also more broadly in relation to quality, environmental standards, and integration into a wider neighbourhood and community which can help to keep people healthy and active for longer and reduce loneliness and isolation.

Age-Friendly Housing: Future Design for Older People is therefore a vitally important resource for those engaged in thinking about and delivering housing for older people. It sets out the key challenges and practical considerations, and exemplifies through excellent case studies what the very best housing for older people looks like across a range of different approaches and tenures. I hope that this book will be read by everyone with an interest in housing for older people. If we are to deliver housing which can help us to enjoy and celebrate living for longer, we need to use every tool at our disposal and this book is a powerful contribution.

Helen Hayes MP
Member of Parliament for Dulwich and West Norwood

Preface

It is almost ten years since the first HAPPI report, *Housing our Ageing Population: Panel for Innovation*, drew attention to the lack of well-designed housing for older people.[2] We were both directly involved in that initiative, which was jointly sponsored by the then Homes and Communities Agency (HCA), then Department of Communities and Local Government (DCLG) and the Department of Health (DoH). That three-way partnership was an important recognition of the interrelationship between health and housing – a synergy that becomes even more important as we get older and, eventually, more 'housebound'. The question asked by the HCA, DCLG and DoH was this:

> *What further reform is needed to ensure that new build specialised housing meets the needs and aspirations of the older people of the future?*

The report was published in late 2009. Did it answer the question? Not entirely, but it has been an extremely effective catalyst for change. Through case studies, here and across Europe, it demonstrated that there is no single housing solution, but many, and that good, contemporary design is not just legitimate, it is part of the answer. It also reminded us that we are the older people of the future; that this issue is not about other people, but about something that will affect us all.

There are now four HAPPI reports and we can expect more. But in many ways this book is the real sequel to the 2009 original, because, it too, focuses on the design of future housing for older people. This time, the question implicit in the title is even broader; the word 'specialised' has been omitted; and it is also about new housing in general. There are two reasons for this. Firstly, the fact that 93% of UK citizens still choose to remain in mainstream (or non-specialised) housing[3], and secondly, the growing realisation that homes need to be flexible; if we design with the future needs of older people in mind, we are likely to produce housing that is desirable for everyone.

Neither of these propositions negates or diminishes the need for specialised housing. On the contrary, it is estimated that there will be a shortfall of 400,000 purpose-built homes for older people by 2035.[4] That makes it more important than ever to devise attractive housing solutions that offer lifestyle choices and access to care, support, security and companionship; particularly as there is a risk that technological advances could mean that loneliness will become a greater problem than mobility constraints for many older people. Whether the 93% are actively choosing to stay put, or simply not choosing to move, is a moot point. Either way, a wider choice of better age-friendly housing options can only be helpful.

The phrase 'older people' felt unsatisfactory when we were writing the first HAPPI report, and seems just as clumsy today. As a relative term, it tells us very little – and who among us is not older than we were? Official thresholds lack consistency. If we are looking for designated housing we only need to be 55; to get a free bus pass we need to be 60; to draw our pension we will soon need to be 70. So far we haven't come up with anything better. While we can comfortably refer to someone as a young person, it is still far less acceptable to refer to someone as an 'old', or even an 'elderly', person. Our perception of someone else's age, and the language we use when referring to them, depends on many factors, including our own age.

Whatever descriptions or criteria we choose, it is clear that older people make up a very significant proportion of the population and that our needs and aspirations do not suddenly converge because of age. In this book, we suggest that age-friendly design, including the use of emerging technologies, should be intrinsic to the way that we think about all the living environments we create, as we continue to explore and expand the range of specialised and bespoke options that could help us live and age well for longer.

We have drawn on many publications, and sought specific insights from a number of experts. Academics, researchers, organisations, health professionals, architects, technical experts and others have generously offered their knowledge, opinions, experience and examples of their work.

These diverse contributions are woven into a background narrative that will be easily accessible to a wide audience. We aim to provide a context for design, consider current and emerging solutions alongside practical guidance, stimulate new ways of thinking and suggest some priorities for the future. The text is illustrated with examples and case studies – inspiring evidence of the diverse range of housing that is becoming available to older people. The majority are UK projects; not only to ensure cultural relevance, but also because they rival some of the best developments found anywhere in the world.

We are extremely grateful to all those who have helped to make this publication possible by providing information and illustrations of exemplary architecture and sharing their professional knowledge, insight and experience of this diverse sector. We hope that this book will inspire everyone involved with the design of homes and neighbourhoods to respond to the growing needs and aspirations of our ageing population here in the UK, and beyond.

We also wish to thank Ginny Mills, Jane Rogers and Daniel Culver at RIBA Publishing for their advice and guidance, Belle Mundy, Zoe Mercer, the external reviewers for their comments and suggestions, and Lois Beech at the Housing LIN and Rose Marshall at Levitt Bernstein, for their support behind the scenes.

Julia Park and Jeremy Porteus

About the authors

JULIA PARK

As an experienced architect and head of housing research at Levitt Bernstein, Julia combines many years of practical design work with a large body of research. She has written numerous design guides, reports and publications, often in collaboration. She co-authored the first HAPPI report in 2009, and the National Housing Federation's *Housing Standards Handbook: A Good Practice Guide to Design Quality for Affordable Housing Providers*, in 2016.

Julia regularly speaks at conferences, contributes to seminars and sits on working groups. During 2012–13, she was seconded to the Department of Communities and Local Government to assist with its review of housing standards, reflecting on that experience in her book, *One Hundred Years of Housing Space Standards, What Now?*, in 2017. She delivered the national RIBA CPD course on accessible housing in 2013–14, chairs the RIBA Housing Group and is a Mayor's Design Advocate for London.

JEREMY PORTEUS

Jeremy is a national expert in housing for older people. He set up the Housing LIN (Learning and Improvement Network) in 2004 while working as the 'Change Agent' at the Department of Health, and was responsible for implementing the government's £300 million capital programme for extra care housing for older people. The Housing LIN has been independent of government since 2011 and has grown to be an extremely popular professional networking forum; bringing together over 40,000 housing, health and social care practitioners in England and Wales to showcase innovative housing solutions for an ageing population.

Jeremy chaired the then Homes and Communities Agency Vulnerable and Older People Advisory Group from 2010–16, and is vice-chair of the Housing and Ageing Alliance. He has been heavily involved in the HAPPI reports, and is secretariat to the All Party Parliamentary Group on Housing and Care for Older People inquiry reports (HAPPI 2, 3 and 4). He writes regular blogs and thought-leadership pieces, and worked with the RIBA research team on their 2014 literature review of design for an ageing population. As a fellow of the National Institute for Health Research, he participates in a number of academic and knowledge transfer projects.

1.0 Introduction

Getting old remains a conundrum. None of us wants to die but few of us look forward to being old. This opening chapter provides a context for addressing the challenge of how we can continue to live well as we live longer. Having set out the scale of the challenge, it looks at some perceptions of ageing, and the physical and cognitive effects of getting older, as a useful starting point for design.

A brief history of housing for older people reminds us that progress has been painfully slow. For centuries, older people with limited means relied on almshouses when they could no longer manage alone. Real change began about a hundred years ago, and more recently, the HAPPI project made its mark, pointing out that opportunity is often the corollary to challenge. The concept of inclusive design is discussed, followed by a brief overview of recent government policy.

1.1 The challenge

CHANGING DEMOGRAPHICS

Across the world, demography is changing. The most significant factors are lower birth rates and longer lifespans. The average household size in England is now only 2.3 people, compared with 4.8 at the start of the 20th century.[5]

Current average life expectancy in the UK is 83 for women and 79 for men. In 1901 it was 49 and 45 respectively.[6] There is some evidence that this is levelling off, due in part to the relatively unhealthy lifestyles of many in the western world, but the number of UK citizens expected to be 85 or over is projected to rise to 3 million by 2030; the number aged 65 or over, to 15 million.[7] Much has been made of this in the media and we see it for ourselves, but as a society, and as a profession, we have been slow to react, particularly in terms of planning for the implications for housing, health and social care.

The challenge is how to live well in later life. Generalisations are dangerous, but research backs up what most of us instinctively feel; we want to remain active, useful members of a community and retain as much control over our lives as possible.[8] 'Control' has often been interpreted as a dogged determination to remain independent, but this is somewhat unfair. On the whole, we want to help ourselves as much as we reasonably can, we recognise when we need help or support and we are grateful when these are provided in an appropriate way.

But the cost of care and support remains a pressing concern. Saving and planning ahead remain difficult because we are so much better at staying alive than we used to be. Many of the diseases and conditions that used to be fatal can now be managed for many years with better care, medication and technology.

> Current average life expectancy in the UK is 83 for women and 79 for men. In 1901 it was 49 and 45 respectively.

> ...having bought and personalised our 'castle', we like to stay in it and pull up the drawbridge.

THE ROLE OF HOUSING

Housing has a fundamental role to play in helping us live well for longer. It is not just about the home we occupy, but also about the place in which we live, who we live with and who we live close to. Culturally, we are possibly more territorial than most of our European neighbours; the UK has traditionally been a nation of homeowners and house dwellers, not renters or apartment leaseholders. We like to put up fences to define and protect what we consider to be 'ours', and, having bought and personalised our 'castle', we like to stay in it and pull up the drawbridge.

Couples tend to manage to live well independently for longer than those who live alone. This is not surprising; love and companionship are enormously comforting in themselves; and knowing that someone is there to help when we need it can make all the difference – even if they are frail too.

Until very recently, our housing options in later life were limited; stay put, move in with a son or daughter, uproot to sheltered housing (often on the advice of worried family or friends) or, in a worst-case scenario, to residential or nursing care. With so few choices, and often none of them ideal, it has been easier not to think about it. And so we stay put, typically not moving until we lose our partner, experience a serious fall, or a sharp decline in our health or mobility. Suddenly we find ourselves moving from necessity, not from choice, and often when we are least able to cope with it – at a crisis point. We watch our parents and grandparents make this mistake, and yet repeat it ourselves.

POSITIVE MOVES

The process of turning that around, making positive choices and being proactive rather than reactive, has begun. Housing choices for older people are broadening all the time. We are starting to see options that represent a positive lifestyle choice rather than a 'least worst option', for couples as well as singles, and care homes are increasingly offering a good quality of life to those with higher levels of need.

Having taken that all-important first step by beginning to contemplate moving, deciding whether to live in a home of our own or move to specialised housing is the first big dilemma we face. It will be influenced by where we want to live, what is available, and what the local area has to offer in terms of wider facilities. If we decide to live with others, does it have to be a binary choice between family and strangers, or could we live with friends, or other people with similar interests? Could groups of older people live well alongside groups of young people – are there intergenerational synergies that we have barely begun to explore?

'Co-living' is a term we rarely used or understood ten years ago. Partly through necessity and partly through more relaxed attitudes, our cultural reluctance to share space in non-family situations is dissipating. To date, this has been more obvious among the young; the lack of affordable housing means that many professionals now find themselves flat-sharing into their 30s or 40s – particularly in London and other major cities. Though often enjoyable, it tends not to be through choice. The ultimate goal for most young sharers is a home of their own – co-living has been a stepping stone, not an end in itself.

For the majority of older people, the experience of co-living would work in reverse. They will have owned or rented a home for most of their lives – probably a house, not an apartment. For many, that remains the priority, but for a growing number of others, the potential to live with friends and experience mutual support and companionship makes some form of sharing an attractive proposition.

One very obvious consequence of an ageing population is the increased demand for health and social care. While arguments about who, and how, we pay for it preoccupy our politicians, it is in all our interests to mitigate the cost and become more resilient – to stay as healthy, active and independent as we can, and to help each other. Given that so little of our existing housing stock is age-friendly, new housing that is practical, accessible, affordable and beautiful, and destigmatises growing old, has a pivotal role to play. It isn't one type of housing, but many, it will evolve over time and some models will prove more successful than others, but there will be common ingredients.

PERCEPTIONS OF AGEING

Ideas about what it means and how it feels to be old, and how others see us, are still evolving. A European Social Survey, conducted in 2009, found that perceptions of 'old age' vary considerably between countries. In the UK, old age is perceived to begin at 59 – the second youngest of the countries surveyed. Youth is perceived to end at 35 – again earlier than most other countries[9] (see Figure 1 overleaf).

Although interesting, it ignores the fact that ageing is a continuum rather than an event, and that we spend a large (arguably an increasing) part of our lives in 'middle age'. Nonetheless, there is resonance in the observation that:

There is a way in which older age can often bring with it a growing sense of marginalisation, of being overlooked, of being somehow less visible, made to feel less relevant.[10]

> ... does it have to be a binary choice between family and strangers, or could we live with friends, or other people with similar interests?

Figure 1: Perceived age at which youth ends and old age starts

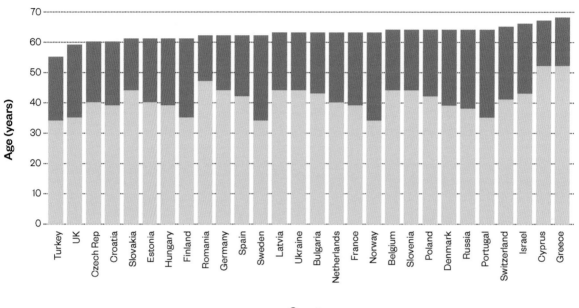

Perception of life stage transition:

End of youth

Start of old age

Survey of 54,988 people aged 15+ across Europe

VIEWPOINT | Mary Evans reflects on change and continuity

Thinking about our 'old' age is for many, if not most people, frightening and very often without any clear models to follow. Yes, there are the endlessly cheerful Saga advertisements of happy couples on Danube cruises but the point that we might notice about these advertisements – apart from the wealth and the whiteness of the couples – is that the people are getting away from real life and presumably their homes.

So what we are all too often presented with in these pictures of old age, is that a happy old age is one where we get away from our previous lives, whereas it is actually our previous lives that are most likely to provide us with forms of happiness and health. Recognising this is part of the reality of old age, and how we live it, is what we have to embrace. Given that for most people mobility, sociability and income are going to decrease in old age, where and how to live takes on greater importance. And, of course, central to these concerns is that of one's residence.

Refusing to think about this key question very often emerges from that understandable aspect of ageing in which we refuse to acknowledge the condition itself. It may seem, to many people, sensible to stay in the same house because it provides familiarity, community and the continuation of previous patterns of life: the rituals of household and garden tasks at certain times of the year, the association of those rituals with people no longer present. All this forms a comfort blanket against loss.

But this comfort blanket can become a straitjacket in which people become penalised for their often single-handed efforts to retain continuity. Housing once appropriate for more than one or two people becomes a costly, tiresome and repetitive burden in which the dominant emotion becomes that of anxiety. The UK, for all kinds of reasons, has recently become a country obsessed with the material value of housing. This general obsession often fuels our refusal to think about housing in a way that might benefit and enrich many more lives, especially those of older people. That way is to think about housing, especially for the elderly, as the bricks and mortar which support and allow two crucial social possibilities: interaction with others and being of value to others.

A greater imagination about housing for the elderly might curtail several of those common fears about old age: being a burden, forgotten and alone. It is impossible to challenge those fears simply by argument and persuasion: but imagining and creating forms of housing that connect people could show that there are ways of living in 'old' age, which maintain the best of the past. Connections with others can be – literally and metaphorically – built into our lives.

Mary Evans, retired Centennial Professor at the Gender Institute, London School of Economics.

> ...this comfort blanket can become a straitjacket in which people become penalised for their often single-handed efforts to retain continuity.

> Connections with others can be – literally and metaphorically – built into our lives.

1.2 The physiology of ageing

A PROFESSIONAL OVERVIEW

 INSIGHT | Andrew Crowther summarises the typical health effects of ageing that can inform design

Ageing is a normal phenomenon, affecting our body and our mind. Many senior citizens lead active, often sporty lives, but most will experience age-related problems that make it more difficult to keep active. Perhaps the most obvious is the lack of energy. After the age of 70 there is a natural decline in the strength of muscle power. The average 'fit' pensioner will have lost muscle bulk and notice reduced physical ability, more difficulty climbing stairs, balancing, manoeuvring and moving quickly.

Poor balance may be due to reduced vision, defective balance organs, or loss of proprioceptive receptors (position sensors in muscles and joints, connected to the brain by the finest of the peripheral nerves). As the fibres wear out over time, the brain is unable to locate the limb in space and we may stumble. When walking, we spend half the time balancing on one leg. If our balance is not good we tend to shuffle rather than pick our feet up, and therefore trip more easily.

Eyesight is just as important as the position sensors. Test this yourself by standing on one leg (usually no problem) but then close your eyes. Most people tend to wobble then stumble. Some degree of sight loss is inevitable as we age, and cataracts or macular degeneration can further reduce our vision. The balance organs close to the inner ear in the skull, the semi-circular canals, depend

on very fine hairs which wear out in time; resulting in giddiness which increases the risk and the fear of falling. These progressive problems often mean that extra support will be needed when moving about. Hearing loss is to be expected too.

We are all more likely to succumb to illness as we age. Common diseases that affect mobility include osteoporosis and cardiovascular disease. Inactivity leads inevitably to thinning of the bone structure, resulting in fractures of limb bones or vertebrae in the spine. A fall or a sudden jolt may be enough to fracture a crumbling bone, so preventing falls is particularly important in later life.

Our lifestyle may lead to damage to the heart and blood vessels, made worse by smoking and obesity. Too much exertion can bring on angina or a heart attack, but even mild damage to heart and blood vessels will slow us down, and blocked arteries can lead to amputation. Lifts, labour saving devices and wheelchairs often become necessary.

Poor blood supply to the brain can lead to damage in the form of strokes or dementia, of which there are several types. Vascular dementia progresses in stops and starts, and Alzheimer's disease, which may start at a young age, causes distressing loss of short-term memory. Visual cues, such as colour-coded

doors, can help us remember where we are when brain function deteriorates.

Arthritis, or inflammation of the joint linings, also takes many forms. Osteoarthritis may be due to damage inflicted many years earlier, while rheumatoid arthritis, an autoimmune disease, causes the body to destroy its own joint linings. This can be a particularly crippling condition, which brings multiple problems, but we can still maintain a useful and active life, as long as the environment in which we spend our time is safe and supportive.

Despite taking all sensible precautions, just a simple urinary infection can confine us to home and make us ill. This and many other conditions may mean we need to use wheelchairs or Zimmer frames, which need wider doors and hallways, and easily become extra hazards in crowded spaces. Perhaps most importantly, illness, memory loss, incontinence and falls can all damage our confidence, setting off a downward spiral of anxiety, inactivity, isolation and dependency. Our lifestyles and our living environments can do a great deal to allow us to live longer, healthier and happier lives.

Andrew Crowther spent 34 years in General Practice in a Gloucestershire market town. He is a magistrate and chairman of the local Abbeyfield House care home.

1.3 The origins of housing for older people

HOSPITALS, ALMSHOUSES AND COLLEGES

Until the early Middle Ages, hospitals were the only option for older people who were no longer able to live at home. St Peter's Hospital in York, founded by King Athelstan in 936, is the first known example of an almshouse, or 'charitable residence for older people'. The earliest surviving example is St Cross Hospital in Winchester, which dates from 1133.

The major expansion in the charitable provision of housing for older people began in northern Europe in the mid-14th century. By the middle of the 1500s, there were roughly 800 medieval hospitals spread across the country, but following the dissolution of the monasteries, only a handful remained. These were refounded on secular lines, and rebuilt in the new 'domestic collegiate' style.

Largely confined to England, Germany and the Low Countries, this divergence between northern and southern Europe continues. In many parts of southern Europe, purpose-built housing is relatively uncommon

↑ Typical English almshouse from the 18th century.

⬆ Similar almshouse models exist across northern Europe; this example is in the suburbs of Copenhagen.

and older people are still usually cared for within extended family groups.

An outbreak of the Black Death in England, in 1348, triggered rapid growth in the provision of almshouses. Some, such as Corpus Christi College in Cambridge, were academic institutions, but many were set up for purely charitable reasons – to provide for those who could no longer look after themselves.

Traditional almshouses have a distinctive form and character. Typically small, two storey houses with arched front doors and tall chimneys, linked to form terraces or three-sided courtyards, they convey a sense of place and a grandeur that belies their essential modesty of scale and purpose. There are still 1,700 almshouse charities in the UK today, a testament to the enduring quality of a successful housing typology.

WORKHOUSES AND ASYLUMS

In Tudor times, parliament passed the first of the 'Poor Laws', which paved the way for the public 'poor houses', later known as 'workhouses'. Relatively few were built over the next 200 years though almshouses continued to flourish. When the industrial revolution led to mass migration into towns, urban poverty became a major problem. The Poor Law Amendment Act of 1834 initiated a huge programme of workhouse building; each parish was obliged to build one. These grim institutions imposed a harsh regime on what were seen as the 'undeserving poor' but were often the only accommodation available to older people. This continued to be the case until the final closure of workhouses in the late 1940s.

From 1845, each county was required to have an 'asylum'. Estimates suggest that over the 19th century, the number of patients institutionalised because of mental illness grew from 1,000 to 100,000 in the UK.

This was due in part to increased life expectancy that led to a corresponding increase in dementia. In effect, these institutions, including the ring of huge asylums around London, provided a further form of housing for older people, arguably worse than the workhouses.

NURSING AND RESIDENTIAL CARE HOMES

Private nursing homes began to appear at the start of the 20th century. These were usually smallish institutions; around ten beds in a large house, converted and extended for the purpose. They now range considerably in size but the essential characteristics of these early 'homes' are still evident: residents occupy a room (usually under a licence) and have access to on-site care and support, day and night. Staff help with washing, dressing, eating and so on. In nursing homes, there is also access to on-site 24-hour medical care from a qualified nurse. Interestingly, nursing homes are the only form of accommodation for older people that remain internationally widespread, including in southern Europe.

SHELTERED AND RETIREMENT HOUSING

Towards the end of the 19th century, local authorities and philanthropists such as George Peabody began building large quantities of social housing. This led to a significant improvement in general housing standards for the working classes. Landlords gradually realised that many tenants whose children had left home were continuing to occupy family houses and flats, and not always managing well. Some organisations began to build smaller flats and bungalows for their older tenants (usually 55 and over), and this marked the start of sheltered housing. The first retirement villages, funded by charitable organisations, date back to a similar period.

→ Bungalows at Whiteley Retirement Village, Walton-on-Thames, Surrey.

↑ The formal layout of Whiteley Village, as seen from above.

Built mainly by local authorities, housing associations and charities for people on lower incomes, sheltered housing became widespread throughout the UK from the late 1960s to early 1980s. The 1969 'Ministry of Housing and Local Government circular 82/69' set standards for two main categories of provision.[11] Category 1 sheltered housing was intended for relatively independent people; the dwellings could be flats or bungalows, while wardens, communal facilities and lifts were optional. Category 2 schemes had to provide more specialised flats, a resident warden service, a communications system, a lift and communal facilities – all 'under one roof'. A further type, offering greater support (Category 2.5 or 'very sheltered'), became the precursor to extra care housing. Unlike almshouses, in which residents are solely dependent upon the goodwill of the administering trustees, sheltered housing provides security of tenure through a formal occupancy agreement.

← Typical sheltered housing from the late 20th century, Tewkesbury, Gloucestershire.

In the mid-1970s, demand was identified for a private sector equivalent to sheltered housing. Two particular companies dominated in the UK market, catering for two different income and age profiles. McCarthy and Stone built blocks of flats in prominent town centre locations, selling primarily to middle income couples in their early 80s, while English Courtyard concentrated on village schemes, based on medieval almshouse precedents but aimed at higher income purchasers, typically ten years younger.

In the late 1980s, many sheltered housing schemes were transferred to housing associations. In 1989, the NHS and Community Care Act laid the foundations for the current policy to support older people in their own homes, in a move away from institutional provision. Much of the original sheltered housing stock is now outdated and has proved difficult to upgrade (see p 52).

Homes for the Third Age, published in 1997 (commissioned by Hanover Housing Association, in conjunction with Brighton University, and funded by the then Housing Corporation) marked the start of extra care housing as we currently understand it – a 'home for life' with on-site access to care and support.[12] Discussed in subsequent chapters, it is now the most common form of new-build specialised housing provision for older people. Overall provision of specialised housing for older people peaked in 1989, when more was built for sale than for rent; 2016 saw an equal split.[13]

Figure 2: Retirement and extra care housing units built by year in the UK

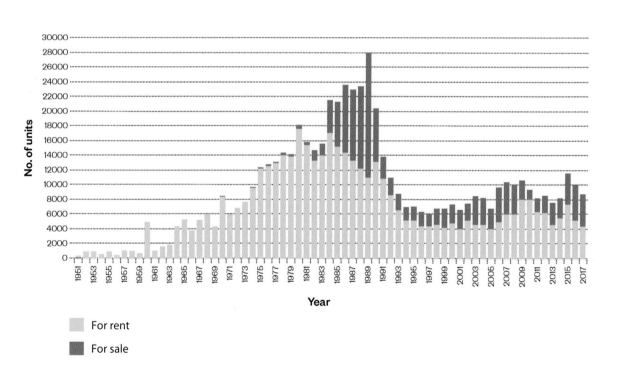

For rent

For sale

1.4 Building on the HAPPI project

UNDERSTANDING THE OPTIONS

The 2009 HAPPI report was possibly the first publication to feature examples of age-friendly housing that most of us could imagine actively choosing to live in. The range of developments was considerable, and the descriptions confusing. A hexagon diagram in the second report organised the options under three broad headings (see below).

The level of care that each is intended to provide increases from left to right. Although not strictly housing, the third column reminds us that older people can spend a considerable amount of time in institutional environments; particularly those who choose to remain in mainstream housing.[14]

↓ FIGURE 3. Range of current age-friendly housing options identified in HAPPI report.

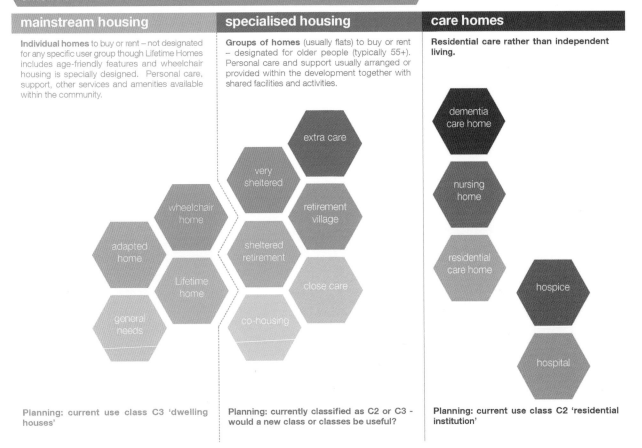

extent of HAPPI influence

mainstream housing

Individual homes to buy or rent – not designated for any specific user group though Lifetime Homes includes age-friendly features and wheelchair housing is specially designed. Personal care, support, other services and amenities available within the community.

specialised housing

Groups of homes (usually flats) to buy or rent – designated for older people (typically 55+). Personal care and support usually arranged or provided within the development together with shared facilities and activities.

care homes

Residential care rather than independent living.

extra care

very sheltered

wheelchair home

retirement village

adapted home

sheltered retirement

Lifetime home

close care

general needs

co-housing

dementia care home

nursing home

residential care home

hospice

hospital

Planning: current use class C3 'dwelling houses'

Planning: currently classified as C2 or C3 - would a new class or classes be useful?

Planning: current use class C2 'residential institution'

In theory, we might expect to progress logically though two or three of these typologies as our care needs increase. In reality, life is neither tidy nor predictable. For some, the transition from late middle to old age is a gradual one, but most of us will experience 'ups and downs' and sudden set-backs, often a fall, illness, disease, or bereavement. Our financial situation is also likely to change – for better or worse.

MANAGING UNCERTAINTY

One of the problems with traditional sheltered housing (particularly when wardens were phased out) was that residents were required to leave when their support needs increased; for example, when assessed by local social services as needing care on a daily basis. Given that making even one move is so difficult, the prospect of multiple moves is daunting. Extra care and other forms of housing, which aim to offer a home for life, can accommodate people with a wide range of health and care needs and are therefore the most flexible, often able to meet our needs until we die.

Technically, even full-time domiciliary care can now be delivered to our own home, but in practice this is often expensive and not always easy to arrange. Even with professional help, judging the right point to move on is extremely difficult, and the move itself can be traumatic. As a result, very few of us make the right move at the right time.

Dementia poses unique challenges. Mood and behaviour often become increasingly unpredictable as the debilitating disease progresses, and it may be desirable, or necessary, to consider moving to a specialist dementia facility. Good design remains just as important, arguably more so.

Ørestad Retirement Home and Meadow View (Case Studies 13 and 14) set a very high standard in terms of design quality, and De Hogeweyk (Case Study 15) offers a highly innovative and holistic approach (see also Graadman Haus, p 17).

In most types of specialised housing you are unable to choose who you live with. The fact that cohousing offers an intentional community is undoubtedly one of the attractions for those who embark on what often proves to be a long journey. In Soloinsieme, St Gallen, Switzerland (another HAPPI project), the group of four bright, competent women who conceived the idea, were still meeting over tea and talking about how nice it would be, ten years after first getting together. Having reached their 60s, they decided to recruit an architect. This marked a turning point; together they found a disused embroidery factory, built in 1880 and suitable for conversion into 17 apartments.

Elisabeth Merkt, one of the founding members, explained how the name, 'Soloinsieme', (an invented word that combines two Italian words – 'solo', meaning 'alone', and 'insieme', meaning 'together'), came about, and what it means for her:

Our architect had the idea for Soloinsieme – that means you are alone but you are also together. So if my door is open, everybody can go in. When it is closed, they know that they should stay outside.[15]

… very few of us make the right move at the right time.

Filling the remaining apartments brought unexpected dilemmas. When the architect asked whether he and his wife might move in to one, the women happily agreed but admitted that it hadn't occurred to them that couples might be interested. Somewhat uncomfortably, they realised that they needed to devise a selection process to fill the remaining apartments. Having accepted a slightly younger woman, they found themselves holding their first 'Extraordinary General Meeting' when she revealed she was pregnant. When the HAPPI experts visited in 2009, this delightful building was home to 17 women, one man (the architect) and a four-year-old boy.

↑ Sociable access decks at Soloinsieme double as semi-private open space.

⬆ Communal garden at
New Ground (Case Study 4).

New Ground (Case Study 4) in High Barnet, north London, was facilitated by Hanover Housing Association, an established provider of housing for older people. The gestation period was such that only one of the founding group moved in to the completed development.

Both projects ended well but they demonstrate that time doesn't stand still and that life is unpredictable. In any venture initially intended for 'younger olds' the demographic changes. As the original occupants start to need more care, or die, it can be difficult to attract enough younger recruits to restore the original ethos and maintain a balanced community. It is therefore vital to look ahead, be realistic and establish clear protocols.

⬉ EXAMPLE | Research-based dementia facility

↑ The top-lit street with views out to the courtyard.

Gradmann Haus in Stuttgart, Germany, one of the most inspiring HAPPI case studies, is still recognised as being at the cutting edge of design and care for people with dementia. Informed by academic research, it provides a homely, gently stimulating environment for 24 residents, split into two 'households'. Each cluster is arranged around a central living, eating and cooking area with familiar sights, sounds and smells. Residents are encouraged to participate in food preparation, and mood boards, artifacts and everyday objects animate the top-lit street that connects the various parts of the building, evoking memories of former home-life. Gradmann Haus also provides a day care facility and assisted living accommodation, including apartments for partners and spouses (see pp 34–36).

i INFO | The HAPPI design principles [16]

1 The new retirement homes should have generous internal space standards, with potential for three habitable rooms and designed to accommodate flexible layouts.

2 Care is taken in the design of homes and shared spaces, with the placement, size and detail of windows, and to ensure plenty of natural light, and to allow daylight into circulation spaces.

3 Building layouts maximise natural light and ventilation by avoiding internal corridors and single-aspect flats, and apartments have balconies, patios, or terraces with enough space for tables and chairs as well as plants.

4 In the implementation of measures to ensure adaptability, homes are designed to be 'care ready' so that new and emerging technologies, such as telecare and community equipment, can be readily installed.

5 Building layouts promote circulation areas as shared spaces that offer connections to the wider context, encouraging interaction, supporting interdependence and avoiding an 'institutional feel', including the imaginative use of shared balcony access to front doors and thresholds, promoting natural surveillance and providing for 'defensible space'.

6 In all but the smallest developments (or those very close to existing community facilities), multipurpose space is available for residents to meet, with facilities designed to support an appropriate range of activities – perhaps serving the wider neighbourhood as a community 'hub', as well as guest rooms for visiting friends and families.

7 In giving thought to the public realm, design measures ensure that homes engage positively with the street, and that the natural environment is nurtured through planting new trees and hedges, the preservation of mature planting, and providing wildlife habitats as well as colour, shade and shelter.

8 Homes are energy-efficient and well insulated, but also well ventilated and able to avoid overheating by, for example, passive solar design, the use of native deciduous planting supplemented by external blinds or shutters, easily operated awnings over balconies, green roofs and cooling chimneys.

9 Adequate storage is available outside the home together with provision for cycles and mobility aids, and that storage inside the home meets the needs of the occupier.

10 Shared external surfaces, such as 'home zones', that give priority to pedestrians rather than cars, and which are proving successful in other countries, become more common, with due regard to the kinds of navigation difficulties that some visually impaired people may experience in such environments.

THE HAPPI LEGACY

The HAPPI reports identify the barriers that continue to prevent housing for older people from becoming widely available. The first report made recommendations for 12 bodies or organisations. These included national and local government, funding authorities, housing associations, house-builders and professional bodies, such as the RIBA. Some of the recommendations have been adopted and others are still gaining traction.

Successive governments have made extensive reference to the HAPPI project, and the National Planning Policy Framework (NPPF) and National Planning Policy Guidance (NPPG) stress the need to meet the housing needs of older and disabled people (see pp 22–25). Many local authorities now include, or reference, the ten good practice design principles enshrined in the first HAPPI report, in local planning policy and guidance. Homes England (formerly the Homes and Communities Agency (HCA)) and the Greater London Authority (GLA) cite them in their funding criteria.

In 2010, the HCA began sponsoring a new category (the 'HAPPI Award') in the prestigious, annual Housing Design Awards.[17] In 2013, Lime Tree Court (Case Study 7) an innovative, multigenerational scheme in Clapton, London, with three distinct clients, won awards in both the mainstream and HAPPI categories; evidence that high quality, contemporary design can, and should, be age-neutral.

HAPPI was open about its multiple aims. While the main agenda was to improve the lives of older people by providing better, more suitable housing options, the report was also clear that there are consequential benefits for all of us. Encouraging downsizing (or 'rightsizing') frees up badly needed family homes and has enormous potential to reduce the cost of health and social care (see DWELL p 100 and pp 102–105). Many other studies confirm this and *Opportunity Knocks*,[18] published by ILC-UK in 2014, provides compelling examples of the commercial advantages of designing general products with older people in mind (see pp 108–111).

1.5 The value of inclusive design

DECIDING WHERE TO DRAW THE LINE

The concept of inclusive design – creating an environment that works for everyone – is one of many unattainable goals that are nonetheless worth striving for. In doing so, we must accept that we will have to draw a line that falls short of ideal, and that meeting the needs of one demographic group may sometimes disadvantage another. Shared surface road treatments are an example; barrier-free for wheelchair users, they can be difficult for people with sight loss.

When it comes to new housing, setting minimum standards that rise over time, coupled with plenty of choice, is a more pragmatic and effective approach than expecting every home to cater for all needs. Given that every home we build today should last at least as long as we do (roughly a hundred years), it is inevitable that the vast majority will, at some point, be occupied by someone aged 75 or above. Age-friendly housing should therefore become the norm rather than the exception; acknowledged as an important step towards universal design but still not

> The human impact of inclusive design must be at the heart of the design process.

At its core, inclusive design is about equality; founded on the premise that everyone should have a right to access barrier-free environments. The concept was inspired by the civil rights movement, and uses the social model of disability. This model suggests that people are disabled by economic, environmental and cultural barriers, rather than by physical, sensory or intellectual 'impairments'. This distinction is important; if people can be disabled or excluded by design they can also be enabled and included by design that is aware of diverse needs.[i]

Design Council CABE (Commission for Architecture and the Built Environment) describes five principles of inclusive design:

1. Place people at the heart of the design process.
2. Acknowledge diversity and difference.
3. Offer choice where a single design solution cannot accommodate all users.
4. Provide for flexibility in use.
5. Provide buildings and environments that are convenient and enjoyable to use for everyone.[ii]

These principles are intended to respond to what people need and want, as well as being flexible. They promote the design of spaces that are safe, convenient and inclusive, regardless of age, gender, mobility, ethnicity or other factors. The majority of accessible and adaptable features have intergenerational, multi-user appeal; wider doorways not only make homes accessible to wheelchair users, they also benefit families with pushchairs, and facilitate furniture moving.

Designing for older people

Inclusive design has clear benefits for older people – particularly when applied to housing and the built environment. The Government Office for Science reports that in mid-2014, the average age exceeded 40 for the first time. By 2040, nearly one in seven people are projected to be aged over 75.[iii] To be credible, long-term housing and planning strategies must therefore consider the challenges and requirements of an ageing population.

As we age, we are likely to develop physical, sensory or cognitive impairments not experienced in earlier life. There are now 850,000 people with dementia in the UK, with numbers set to rise to more than one million by 2025.[iv] As dementia is also now the most common reason for entering residential care for over-65s, design that includes people with dementia is likely to help more older people remain in their own home for longer.[v] Advances in technology, including smart technologies in the home, are also providing significant benefits for a wide range of demographics, including older people.

Looking to the future

Access and inclusion is a continuous journey. In a world of increasingly evolving technologies, inclusive design should be continually re-evaluated and reinvented in order to respond to the ever-changing environment and society that we live in. It must extend beyond homes to the communities that surround them. Accessible environments are crucial to allowing everyone to participate in community life, and enjoy the best possible quality of life regardless of age.

Although the value of accessible and adaptable housing is often evidenced in financial terms – through the health and social care 'savings' made by easing delayed discharge from hospital, for example – the benefits extend far beyond the economic. More attention has recently been given to the extent to which housing impacts on happiness and wellbeing.

This is particularly important when addressing loneliness and isolation in older people. Homes that are accessible (or at least 'visitable') can enable older and disabled people to maintain relationships, and increase independence and physical activity. Inclusive design can allow grandparents to play an active role in their grandchildren's lives, ensure that friends and family are able to visit, and that they have the freedom to visit them too. These simple acts can have an immensely positive impact on physical and mental health and well-being, and their value should be recognised.

While inclusive design can future-proof our housing stock, in order for this to be truly effective, diverse requirements must be considered as an integral part of the design process, rather than dealt with retrospectively. The human impact of inclusive design must be at the heart of the design process.

Christina McGill, Head of Communication at Habinteg, and Jean Hewitt, Director of Habinteg's consultancy team, Centre for Accessible Environments.

Notes

i   J. Clarkson, R. Coleman, S. Keates, and C. Lebbon (eds.), *Inclusive design* (London: Springer, 2003), pp 1–10.

ii   Design Council, 2006, http://www.designcouncil.org.uk/sites/default/files/asset/document/the-principles-of-inclusive-design.pdf

iii Government Office for Science, 2016, https://www.gov.uk/government/uploads/system/uploads/attachment_data/file/535187/gs-16-10-future-of-an-ageing-population.pdf, p 6.

iv   Alzheimer's Society, 2017 https://www.alzheimers.org.uk/info/20027/news_and_media/541/facts_for_the_media

v   Alzheimer's Society, 2007 https://www.alzheimers.org.uk/download/downloads/id/270/home_from_home_full_report.pdf

◥ EXAMPLE | Inclusive design in practice

Parkside (Case Study 1), a small, mixed-use, mainstream development in Matlock, Derbyshire, has attracted older purchasers simply by providing inclusively designed, age-friendly accommodation in an excellent location with a range of facilities on the doorstep. For example, a cafe and hairdressing salon have taken space at the base of the building.

i INFO | The scope of Lifetime Homes criteria

1. Parking (width or widening capability)
2. Approach to dwelling from parking (distance, gradients and widths)
3. Approach to all entrances
4. Entrances
5. Communal stairs and lifts
6. Internal doorways and hallways
7. Circulation space
8. Entrance-level living space
9. Potential for entrance-level bed space
10. Entrance-level WC and shower drainage
11. WC and bathroom walls
12. Stairs and potential through-floor lift in dwellings
13. Potential for fitting of hoists and bedroom/bathroom relationship
14. Bathrooms
15. Glazing and window handles
16. Location of service controls.

1.6 The impact of government policy

LIFETIME HOMES

The notion that housing should be accessible to older and disabled people is a remarkably recent idea. Lifetime Homes, 16 design criteria developed to make homes more easily adaptable for 'lifetime use', was conceived by the Helen Hamlyn Foundation and developed by the Joseph Rowntree Foundation (JRF) and Habinteg Housing Association in 1991. Influenced by this initiative, Part M of the Building Regulations, *Access to and Use of Buildings*, was extended to include housing in 1999.[20]

Though the Part M provisions were (and still are) basic, they were an important first step towards age-friendly housing being seen as a mainstream concept. Lifetime Homes slowly gained traction through the planning system and, in 2004, the GLA made it mandatory for all new London homes. In 2008, the Labour Government announced its intention to, 'work towards all new homes being built to Lifetime Homes Standards by 2013'.

LIFETIME NEIGHBOURHOODS

Lifetime Homes, Lifetime Neighbourhoods: A National Strategy for Housing in an Ageing Society, was also published in 2008.[21] Produced by the DCLG in conjunction with the DoH and the DWP, it responded to a discussion paper, *Towards Lifetime Neighbourhoods: Designing sustainable communities for all*, written for DCLG by the International Longevity Centre UK (ILC-UK).[22] The aim was to extend the concept of accessible, inclusive design to whole neighbourhoods, complete with a full range of community services and facilities.

The Top of the Ladder, a 2013 report by Demos, explains the thinking behind it:

… it (Lifetime Homes, Lifetime Neighbourhoods) described two nations in old age… increasingly polarised by housing wealth… it promised to build more mainstream and specialised homes for older people over the next three years, including increased investment in social housing and equity sharing.

It also outlined a new approach to a national housing advice and information service, with strengthened local housing information services, to enable older people to find out about their housing options, whether to stay put or move home, or to consider equity release.

The strategy argued in favour of making it easier and safer for people to stay in their own homes, near their family and neighbours. It also outlined a 'new positive vision' for specialised housing for older people as somewhere they might aspire to live. The Labour Government said it would create 'more homes and more choice', through increased funding for public housing and by encouraging private sector provision through reform of the planning system.[23]

The report also observes that relatively little was achieved following these policy pledges. Commissioning the first HAPPI report proved to be one of the final acts of the last Labour Government before losing power to the 2010 Conservative/Liberal Democrat coalition.

Politicians of all persuasions have always had to tread carefully to avoid being accused of bullying older people out of their under-occupied homes and risk losing 'grey votes'.

Laying the Foundations: A Housing Strategy in England, published in November 2011, was carefully phrased in this respect:

… for some older people a move to a smaller, more accessible and manageable home can also free up much-needed local family housing.[24]

Rejecting Labour's earlier aim to make Lifetime Homes mandatory, the coalition government confirmed that decisions on the number of 'lifetime homes' within each development should, instead, be made at a local level, according to need. The 'new deal' for older people's housing, announced in the strategy, focused mainly on keeping older people independent; living in their own homes (and out of residential care) for as long as possible – barely mentioning specialised retirement housing.[25]

Paragraph 50 of the *National Planning Policy Framework* (NPPF), first published in 2012, requires Local Authorities:

To deliver a wide choice of high quality homes, widen opportunities for home ownership and create sustainable, inclusive and mixed communities, local planning authorities should:

• *plan for a mix of housing based on current and future demographic trends, market trends and the needs of different groups in the community (such as, but not limited to, families with children, older people, people with disabilities, service families and people wishing to build their own homes)…[26]*

2012–15 HOUSING STANDARDS REVIEW

In 2012, the government began a three-year review of housing standards. The aim was to simplify the plethora of local standards that housing developers had claimed were hindering recovery from the 2007–08 global recession. Despite the deregulatory agenda, all parts of the sector expressed a strong preference for any 'rules' considered necessary to be taken into regulation, rather than remain in planning where they were vulnerable to local interpretation.

Acting on this feedback, modified versions of Lifetime Homes and wheelchair housing requirements were taken into Part M of the Building Regulations as 'optional requirements'. Sitting above the existing, mandatory baseline, these two higher levels can now be invoked by local authorities in the proportions required to address local need (see p 92).

In principle, this represents a significant step forward, but in practice, as *National Planning Policy Guidance (NPPG)* makes clear, the optional requirements can only be adopted where it can be shown that this would not jeopardise development viability.[27] The provision of accessible housing therefore remains very patchy; in areas such as north east England, where the housing market is less buoyant, it has proved difficult to invoke the optional requirements, despite above-average levels of need.

In a press release issued on 21 March 2015, the (then) Housing Minister, Brandon Lewis, announced that:

Older people should be given a greater choice where to live during their retirement.

As we get older our housing needs change – I want to be sure that anyone in that situation has a range of options to choose from. No one should feel forced to move out of the home they love just because of their changing circumstances, which is why we've made millions of pounds available to adapt homes for older people.

But I want to see councils doing more, and thinking about building more bungalows and other types of homes to meet the needs of their older residents, so if someone does choose to move the properties are there for them to choose from…[28]

Despite this, and the many publications, select committee inquiries and reports that have been urging successive governments to take steps to increase the supply of age-friendly housing of all types, relatively little action has been taken at national level. However, paragraph 4.42 of *Fixing Our Broken Housing Market*, a white paper published on 8 February 2017, introduced a welcome new measure:

To ensure that there is more consistent delivery of accessible housing, the Government is introducing a new statutory duty through the Neighbourhood Planning Bill on the Secretary of State to produce guidance for local planning authorities on how their local development documents should meet the housing needs of older and disabled people.

Guidance produced under this duty will place clearer expectations about planning to meet the needs of older people, including supporting the development of such homes near local services. It will also set a clear expectation that all planning authorities should set policies using the Optional Building Regulations to bring forward an adequate supply of accessible housing to meet local need. In addition, we will explore ways to stimulate the market to deliver new homes for older people.[29]

The Bill has now been enacted and housing for older people is rising up the political agenda with a number of independent reviews and parliamentary inquiries taking place.

1.7 Summary

Inclusive design, accessible housing, Lifetime Homes and age-friendly housing are all relatively new constructs, despite the fact that we have always grown old. A combination of rapid demographic change, due largely to medical and technological advances, a pension crisis that is unable to deal with the rising cost of health and social care, and recognition that older people have generally been marginalised for too long, has forced us all to think again.

Housing is only part of the issue, but a significant part; we now understand that unsuitable housing is part of the problem, so by implication, suitable housing is part of the solution.

The concept, and the value, of age-friendly housing is now being recognised globally.

Given that is has taken so long to get this far, the rate of current progress and the range of options coming forward are cause for celebration. But it is clear that ideas are still forming and that while policy is starting to move in the right direction, it has so far failed to provide coherent thinking on the interrelationship between housing, health and social care. Until this happens, progress will continue to rely on local authorities to identify and justify the need for housing for older and disabled people, and on individual providers, to choose to address that need. Fiscal uncertainty has lingered in the wake of the 2007–08 global recession and funding for most forms of affordable housing, including specialised housing, has reduced significantly.

Allowing *Lifetime Homes, Lifetime Neighbourhoods* to fade away represents a missed opportunity. One of its legacies, the 2009 HAPPI report, has helped to raise awareness and enthusiasm, and spark action. Significantly, it focused on the benefits of good design, questioning traditional, stereotypical responses. Lessons are being learned and shared, and expectations are rising. What was seen as good enough for older people even ten years ago, now feels barely acceptable, and that upwards trajectory needs to continue in both mainstream and specialised housing of all types and tenure.

> Inclusive design, accessible housing, Lifetime Homes and age-friendly housing are all relatively new constructs, despite the fact that we have always grown old.

> What was seen as good enough for older people even ten years ago, now feels barely acceptable.

2.0 Approaching a new project

This chapter is aimed at clients as well as designers; particularly where managed facilities are envisaged. It takes a more detailed look at the expanding range of options, considers how to go about deciding which course of action to take, and the extent to which planning systems may impact on decision-making and design. It considers a number of different neighbourhood contexts, working with existing buildings, the importance of maintaining social connectivity, and some scenarios that offer specific opportunities.

Whether a local authority, housing association, private developer, charitable body or an individual, every client needs to make a number of strategic decisions before embarking on a new project. A good brief will focus as much on social and organisational issues – how the building should feel, who will live there, how it will be managed, what sort of care and support will be needed – as on the physical spaces required.

2.1 Deciding what type of housing to build

SPOILT FOR CHOICE

While it is desirable to have numerous options, it makes it more difficult to decide what to build. The first choice faced by a housing provider is effectively the same as that we face ourselves – is this specialised or 'age-designated' housing – or is it 'ordinary housing' designed to suit, and therefore to attract, people in later life?

In terms of the homes themselves, there may be little practical distinction, but deciding whether or not to apply care- or age-related eligibility criteria is likely have a significant effect on the resident or customer base. This often relates more to personal preference, background, circumstances and expectation than to objective planning for present or future care needs.

Anecdotal evidence suggests that setting any age limit (even one as low as 55) may, in itself, attract a much older cohort than might otherwise have been the case. The average age of those living in McCarthy and Stone retirement housing is 79, and this rises to 83 in their assisted living schemes.[30] Churchill Retirement Living, which accepts people of 60 and above, describes its typical purchaser as:

A 79-year-old widow moving after her husband has passed away; usually leaving an older, larger house – generally a mid-terrace or semi-detached with two to three bedrooms and a garden – for a one or two bedroom apartment that is close to relatives.[31]

An identified user group can make a scheme easier to design, and the marketing more targeted. A large proportion of those clients who wish to develop specialised housing for sale or rent will be experienced and have their own tried and tested models. Many will have a generic brief and some will have very specific design requirements, often including standard apartment plans. But most have reviewed their approach and the viability of their product range over the last few years; partly in response to changes in revenue funding and Housing Benefit, and partly because the HAPPI project has raised the bar in terms of design quality.

Where age-friendly housing is not intended to be designated or age-restricted, and requirements are not defined, the principles of universal design (see pp 19–21) become particularly important. Most of the HAPPI design principles (see pp 18–19) will also be relevant, as will many of the dementia-friendly considerations (see p 34 and p 36).

EXTRA CARE HOUSING

Extra care, or 'housing with care', (the broad equivalent of 'very sheltered' housing) is now the most common type of specialised housing for older people. There is no formal definition and descriptions vary considerably, but there is general agreement that extra care provides a core set of ingredients, most of which are not provided in typical sheltered housing:

- Purpose-built, accessible building design that promotes independent living and supports people to age in place.
- Fully self-contained properties where occupants have their own front doors, and tenancies or leases which give them security of tenure and the right to control who enters their home.

- Office for use by staff serving the scheme and sometimes the wider community.
- Some communal spaces and facilities.
- Access to care and support services 24 hours a day.
- Community alarms and other assistive technologies.
- Safety and security often built into the design with fob or person-controlled entry.[32]

The absence of a formal definition makes it difficult for potential residents to know what to expect and leads to systemic inconsistencies. Under the planning regime it may be dealt with as Use Class C2 (residential institutions), Use Class C3 (dwelling houses) or occasionally as 'sui generis' (meaning 'of its own type'). This can affect the design standards that apply, the Section 106 requirements imposed (including those for affordable housing), the threshold at which residents are eligible for financial help and many other facets.

As 'extra care' is not a term that has ever featured in the Building Regulations, understanding the technical requirements for the detailed design and construction phases can bring fresh complexity. Many organisations, including the RIBA, have lobbied for a consistent definition and categorisation but no action has yet been taken.[33]

....

Planning Use Classes are being tested by contemporary developments that blur traditional divides between dwellings and care environments, housing and health, public and private.[34]

....

Extra care is usually provided by housing associations and has traditionally been a rental option, but shared ownership has become more common over the last decade and a growing number of schemes are mixed tenure. The emphasis is on meeting need rather than offering a positive lifestyle choice and the name itself can be off-putting, particularly to those with lower care needs. This is a great pity; to care about someone, or to know that someone cares about you, is a privilege. Somewhere along the line, to need care, especially if you have to pay for it, has become a misfortune rather than a natural consequence of enjoying a long life. The same is true of 'support'– this too, has accrued negative connotations in the context of ageing.

Accommodating cultural and gender diversity in housing with care requires particular sensitivity. Social care, such as help with cooking, bathing and dressing, often requires intimate personal contact and frequently involves activities associated with important cultural rituals; many of which are considered to be private. Managing diversity within a mixed cultural group can be particularly difficult but is likely to become easier over time. The sensitive deployment of assistive technology may be helpful (see pp 64–65 and 98–99).[35]

↑ Highwood Mill extra care
development in Horsham,
West Sussex (PRP for Saxon
Weald Housing Association).

RETIREMENT HOUSING

Terms such as 'retirement housing', 'independent living', 'lifestyle housing', 'senior living' and 'third-age housing' are less medicalised and generally aimed at purchasers, though market rental options are becoming available too. Similar to extra care schemes in many respects, they cater for a wider range of budgets. PegasusLife, one of the newer, top-end providers, uses upbeat language and sophisticated, digital marketing techniques to present an enticing, luxurious lifestyle offer to a particular demographic:

Our starting point in everything we do is the people who choose to live in our developments. What will they want to do here? What type and style of service is appropriate? What kind of living environment do we need to create to generate the right atmosphere and give people the experience they're looking for?[36]

Design is extremely high on their agenda and, as documented in HAPPI 3, the ownership business model and code of practice is also worth noting.[37]

⬇ 'Later life living' or 'retirement housing' in Lichfield, Staffordshire, (Case Study 6).

COHOUSING

A form of co-living, this requires a more bespoke design process, as well as a more bespoke product. In almost all cases, it will be the first, and only, building (or buildings) procured by a group of relatively inexperienced people. They will tend to share a strong vision about what they want in principle, but may have very different ideas about what that means in practice. Acquiring a suitable site can be the biggest hurdle and the design process tends to be long and iterative, requiring special skills of the architect.

Reflecting on the design of New Ground (Case Study 4), Pollard Thomas Edwards was impressed by the community ethos:

Senior cohousing fundamentally differs from sheltered housing in that the residents are in active control of managing their community in every way from the earliest stages. Each member is expected to contribute in whatever way they can, making for a real sense of community, and this combats the feelings of isolation and uselessness that affect so many older people living alone.

As this scheme demonstrates, cohousing can be a particularly attractive option for people who share special interests or characteristics. Stonewall Housing Association recently reported that:

Over the past decade, a number of surveys and research papers have identified a significant number of older lesbian, gay, bisexual and transgender (LGBT) people who wish to live in housing settings that are either exclusively or primarily occupied by LGBT people…[38]

RETIREMENT VILLAGES AND CONTINUING CARE RETIREMENT COMMUNITIES

Retirement villages are generally the largest form of developments for older people. A number of American examples comprise over 10,000 homes, while European equivalents typically provide between 90 and 350. All offer extensive non-residential facilities, including shops, leisure and cultural facilities, on a single site. In essence they create a 'self-sufficient community'; a place where everything an older person might reasonably need is on their doorstep. Some are based on the 'home for life' concept, others, described as 'continuing care', provide a range of different types of accommodation through which residents can progress as their needs change. The village concept makes a great deal of practical sense but, for some, implies segregation, rather than integration – a reminder that we all see things differently and make different choices.

Whiteley Village, in Walton-on-Thames, Surrey, created 100 years ago, now provides more than 250 'almshouse bungalows' and offers an active, community style of living. During surveys conducted in 2015 and 2016, 70–75% of residents agreed that:

there was something to share about life there that would be of benefit to others.[39]

Independent research by academics at the Cass Business School found that a woman who arrived at Whiteley in 1960, at the age of 67, could expect to live a further 19.2 years – 4.9 years longer than average. The figure dropped to 3.3 years for the 1980 cohort, but only because of better general living conditions for pensioners.[40]

← On-site shop at Earlsdon Park Retirement Village in Coventry (Nicol Thomas for ExtraCare Charitable Trust).

In practical terms, the bungalows and cottages are now far from ideal for older residents. Relatively small and poorly insulated, many lack step-free access. The sense of community and high standard of the subsidised care and support provided on site account for much of their enduring success (see p 10).

Research by Aston University, commissioned by ExtraCare Charitable Trust, demonstrates the 'health dividend' of extra care villages. It found that a resident's NHS costs reduced by 38% over 12 months, an average saving of £1,114.94 per person per year.[41]

RESIDENTIAL CARE HOMES

Although people can spend many years in care homes, they offer no security of tenure and are formally regarded as institutions rather than housing. Most provide at least 60 beds, often substantially more. The private accommodation is typically a bedroom with an en suite shower, and the cost of meals and care is included in the monthly fee. They are regulated under the Care Standards Act 2000, and subject to national minimum standards drawn up by the Department of Health.

→ Typical care suite.

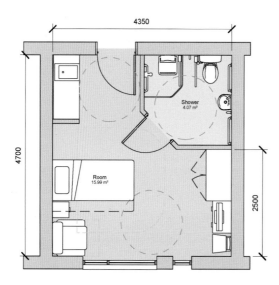

↑ A simple shelf allows residents of Ørestad Retirement Home to personalise and identify the entrance to their apartment.

Very few of these standards relate to design; the most notable is for bedrooms in new developments to be a minimum of 12m² (equivalent to a typical double bedroom).[42] The line between extra care and care homes is ever more blurred. Bedrooms in newer care homes are often grouped into small clusters – each supported by lounge and dining spaces; increasingly care homes are seen as places to live, rather than places to die (see p 17 and Case Study 14).

SPECIALISED DEMENTIA FACILITIES

There are more than 800,000 people in the UK living with some form of dementia – a figure that is expected to rise to 1.7 million by 2051. Dementia already costs the UK economy £26.3 billion each year; more than cancer and heart disease combined.[43] Age-friendly housing should therefore aim to be dementia-friendly too. The Department of Health and the Alzheimer's Society's *Dementia-Friendly Housing Charter* provide general guidance.[44]

ℹ INFO | Principles for dementia-friendly spaces

The Department of Health published Health Building Note 08–02 *Dementia-Friendly Health and Social Care Environments*. Although aimed at health and social care environments, most of the 12 principles, developed from recent research, are relevant to the design of housing and other building types:

1. Provide a safe environment
2. Provide optimum levels of stimulation
3. Provide optimum lighting and contrast
4. Provide a non-institutional scale and environment
5. Support orientation
6. Support wayfinding and navigation
7. Provide access to nature and the outdoors
8. Promote engagement with friends, relatives and staff
9. Provide good visibility and visual access
10. Promote privacy, dignity and independence
11. Promote physical and meaningful activities
12. Support diet, nutrition and hydration.[45]

Many of the measures that help most; clear wayfinding, the grouping of related facilities, good daylight, and fixtures, fittings and controls that are easy to reach and use, are simply sound design principles that work for everyone. Others, such as the use of tonal contrast to make certain doors and features more obvious are also easy to incorporate – either from the start, or when needed.

When designing specifically for older people, it makes sense to go further, and in specialised dementia facilities, further still. When there is an opportunity to design a bespoke home, it is possible to invoke very personal memories.[46]

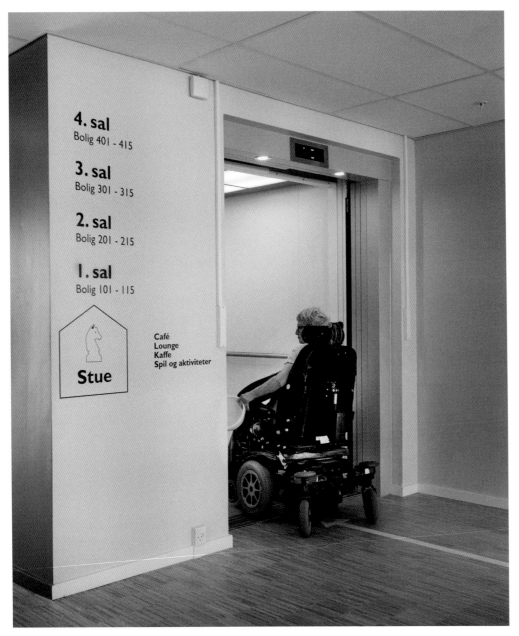

4. sal
Bolig 401 - 415

3. sal
Bolig 301 - 315

2. sal
Bolig 201 - 215

1. sal
Bolig 101 - 115

Stue

Café
Lounge
Kaffe
Spil og aktiviteter

There are more than 800,000 people in the UK living with some form of dementia – a figure that is expected to rise to 1.7 million by 2051. Dementia already costs the UK economy £26.3 billion each year; more than cancer and heart disease combined.

← Clear and intuitive signage in key parts of the communal areas aid navigation.

i INFO | Checklist for dementia-friendly design

When designing new buildings:

- As dementia affects cognitive ability, it is important that the environment is easy to understand and navigate – keep things clear and simple.

- Ensure that environments are not over-stimulating – keep noise levels low, avoid large areas of very bright colour, wallpaper with large patterns, shiny surfaces and mirrors.

- Avoid dead-ends and provide visual clues to aid wayfinding; consider a different colour scheme for every floor level and distinctive artwork or objects, at changes of direction in corridors.

- Provide step-free access throughout every development; ensuring that the maximum change in floor level is 15mm, and that this is managed through a sloping transition section, not a step or bar.

- Choose well designed signs and mount them low: weak neck and shoulder muscles, as well as poor eyesight, mean that the optimal height for signage is approximately 1200mm from floor level.

- Improve safety and understanding by using tonal contrast positively – strong contrast makes things visible (e.g. a dark door handle against a light door), while a lack of contrast makes them invisible.

- Avoid marked tonal contrast where different flooring or paving surfaces meet. People with dementia can struggle with 3D perception and may misinterpret changes in contrast as steps or holes. Many older people with sight impairments will have the same difficulties, regardless of dementia, so this will benefit everyone.

- Similarly, avoid shiny flooring: reflections can be confusing, and may make the floor appear wet.

- Provide higher than normal levels of natural and artificial light – older people generally, and people with dementia in particular, need more light to make sense of their environment and many have significant sight loss.

- Remember that external spaces can be as disabling as internal spaces and their design needs equal attention.

When considering bespoke features or modifications to existing buildings:

- Avoid changing too much; people with dementia may have difficulty adjusting to change.

- As dementia impairs recent memory first, when contemplating changes, consider the person's strongest memories, which are likely to be from their more distant past (e.g. traditional cross-headed taps are likely to recall early home life, and many older people find them easier to use than modern alternatives).

- Focus on design changes that will help people to see where things are and where to go – glass-fronted kitchen cabinets or open shelving make it easier to remember and locate what is needed.

- Provide opportunities for residents living with dementia to personalise the entrance to their apartment. Consider painting the door to match that of their previous home and/or provide a ledge for a well-loved ornament or photograph that evokes long-term memory and helps identify 'home'.

- Inside apartments, specify mirrors that can be easily removed, rather than glued to the walls.

Our understanding of dementia and how to care for people with the disease is evolving fast and a huge amount of research is underway. Naturally, much of this is focused on understanding the causes and finding a cure, but other work is concentrating on improving the lives of people living with the condition. Many academic institutions, notably the University of Stirling, continue to produce valuable evidence, and design professionals are also making important contributions (see p 17).[47]

i INFO | Virtual Reality Empathy Platform (VR-EP)

Software developed by David Burgher of Aitken Turnbull Architects helps designers to experience building environments through the eyes of a fictional person living with dementia. The 'VR-EP' uses special goggles to change visual perception and introduce a range of visual distortions unique to the condition. Burgher explains how the goggles work and some of the potential benefits:

. . . .

There is a haziness, things are less clear, depth of field is reduced so, for example, when looking down a corridor you can't see the end. The software modifies colour too, to increase awareness of dementia perception. A key consideration is colour choices for floors, as some can look like a step causing people living with dementia to lift their leg and fall. There is a significant colour desaturation (with the software) and the level of contrast of an object becomes much more important than the colour…[48]

. . . .

OTHER FACTORS

Inevitably, the decision about what type of housing to build rests very largely with the client. It will be influenced by numerous factors, including the size, nature and location of the site, the local demographic, the proximity to local services and the availability of public transport, the nature of demand and what else already exists, or is planned, in the area.

When specialised or designated housing is proposed, it will often be subject to the vagaries of the planning system (see p 29). Early dialogue with the local authority, concerning the type of development and the Use Class likely to be applied, is important if policy is to help rather than hinder. The availability of capital and revenue funding will also be crucial to ensuring that accommodation is affordable and financially sustainable.

2.2 Integration with the wider community

MOVING IN, NOT MOVING OUT

Most of us want to remain active and useful members of the wider community for as long as possible. Statistically, older people are among the greatest givers of free time. 30% of voluntary work is carried out by people over 65; each spends an average of over 100 hours 'informally volunteering', and more than 55 hours in formal volunteering roles. This is estimated to be worth £10 billion to the UK economy.[49]

. . . .

More than any other group in society, older people are the social glue of most communities.[50]

. . . .

Today's older people are the babies that boomed in the 50s and 60s; often characterised as liberal, sociable and relatively wealthy. This cohort may be retiring in the literal sense, but are more willing to speak up than their parents or grandparents, particularly about how they wish to live. This creates a significant 'pull factor' – demand for the right types of housing in the right places. While many still find the idea of retiring to the country or the coast an attractive proposition, growing numbers are choosing to remain in, or move to, a town or city to take advantage of the social and cultural opportunities.

↓ Multigenerational living at Lime Tree Court (Case Study 7).

Being close to shops, cafés, restaurants, leisure and health facilities encourages activity and interaction. Residents of retirement housing, extra care apartments and care facilities can feel a stronger sense of belonging if they live close to the centre of community.

Sonia Parol, Associate Director, Head of Care and Residential, Urban Edge Architecture

This has implications for the project brief for new age-friendly developments. On the one hand, it may be sensible to provide fewer, or smaller, communal facilities within the development – because they already exist nearby. On the other, it may mean making more of the communal facilities by opening them up to the wider public to create a 'community hub', often able to generate useful revenue through rental income (see pp 65–66). In most towns and cities, there will be scope for both approaches.

INTERGENERATIONAL (OR MULTIGENERATIONAL) HOUSING

Inter- or multigenerational developments achieve the most finely grained, mixed communities. Hanover Housing Association's Lime Tree Court (see p 19 and Case Study 7) combines three distinct housing types and tenures side-by-side in a single building. At one end, there are homes for outright sale, at the other, assisted living homes for older people, and in the centre, shared ownership apartments for the local Orthodox Jewish population. Externally, the building reads as one, only closer inspection reveals the subtle differences that respond to the needs of each group.

➤ EXAMPLE | Multigenerational mainstream suburban house

In 2015, Barratt Homes launched an open competition with a brief to design a set of four speculative suburban house types. They needed to be forward-looking, suitable for use across the country and designed for different household needs. The first was a starter home, the next two were homes for a small and large family, and the fourth a home for different generations.

Levitt Bernstein's shortlisted entry included an L-shaped, multigenerational house with two front doors, designed for a street corner.

Typical site layout showing the multigenerational home on the street corners.

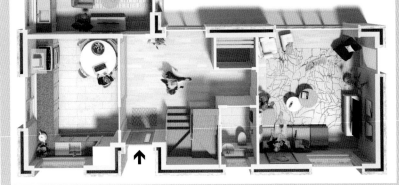

The long side of the L is a family home on two or three storeys, the short side is a single storey, self-contained annexe; designed with granny in mind, it is also suitable for a grown-up son or daughter, lodger, friend or home office. The annexe connects to the hall of the family wing, next to the family kitchen/dining room that forms the knuckle of the plan. For ultimate flexibility, the annexe can easily be fully integrated with the family home.

← Ground floor plan of prototypical multigenerational house.

A recent Dutch model of intergenerational living, in which university students live alongside older people, is inspiring. Known as 'homeshare', the students enjoy cheap rent in return for providing a few, regular hours of practical help (shopping, tidying or reading) or simply companionship, to their older neighbours.[51] A similar scheme is being successfully piloted in Rudolph Seniors Home, Helsinki's largest state care home. Three young people are living among, and engaging with, the older residents, in rooms that are no longer considered suitable for them. Part of a wider, city-funded initiative, 'A Home that Fits', the aim is to ease homelessness, and relieve the social isolation felt by some of the older residents.[52] Here in the UK, several universities are exploring how to develop mutually beneficial living arrangements between alumni and their student populations.

At the micro-level, there are signs that 'granny flats' are making a comeback. Grandparents have certainly been playing a greater role in childcare over the last 15 years or so; they are enjoying many more active, post-retirement years, just as 'stay-at-home mums' become less common, single parenting more prevalent, and nurseries increasingly unaffordable. The bond between grandchildren and grandparents is often extremely strong and different from the parental relationship. Where this works well, it brings three generations closer together.

It is encouraging that volume house-builders see a market for this type of arrangement, which revives an old tradition and combines proximity with independence. While the house may need to be relatively large, it will be effectively home to what otherwise would have been two separate households – a valuable way to ease the housing shortage.

A recent RIBA competition produced a range of other solutions, including a number of purpose-designed pods intended for the rear gardens of existing suburban housing.[53]

As 75% of over-65s are homeowners, and the majority of those are mortgage free, most grandparents would be in a position to contribute to the cost of arrangements such as these.[54]

NEW GARDEN TOWNS AND VILLAGES

Large-scale new developments and urban extensions offer a significant opportunity to create mixed and sustainable neighbourhoods. With the benefit of hindsight and a clean sheet of paper (none of the messy constraints of an existing town that has grown in an ad hoc way), new settlements can combine a wide range of housing typologies with the optimum social and physical infrastructure to create 'a model community'.

It makes a great deal of sense to house older people in the heart of a community, rather than its periphery. Support could be provided by a health and care 'hub' or 'zone' offering GP, dental, ophthalmic, therapy and diagnostic facilities, spaces for dance, music, exercise, IT and learning for the whole community, and providing a base for coordinating social care (see p 20 and p 66). Local school facilities such as ball courts, sports pitches, swimming pools and performance spaces could all be open to the community during the evenings and at weekends, and interaction between young and old encouraged.

Some of these opportunities are being explored in plans for Ebbsfleet Garden City in Kent – the first new town to be designated in the UK for 50 years, the first garden city for 100 years and the largest of the ten Healthy New Town (HNT) pilots – being developed collaboratively through a programme pioneered by NHS England.[55]

EXAMPLE | Derwenthorpe village extension, York

Designed by Studio Partington, Derwenthorpe embodies the ethos and legacy of the client, the Joseph Rowntree Housing Trust. Following the precedent set by the nearby 'model village' of New Earswick, it provides a sustainable framework for an age-friendly community, designed to meet the needs of current and future residents. All 500 homes are built to Lifetime Homes standards and local facilities include schools, nurseries, doctor and dental surgeries, a library and shops.

Heating and hot water are efficiently distributed to the low-energy homes from the centrally located energy centre, which also serves as a community centre accommodating gatherings of up to 50 people. The housing layout is planned to make best use of the existing landscape, including the ancient hedgerows and trees within the site, and SuDs (sustainable drainage systems) and swales have been extensively integrated into the design. The creation of a vibrant, self-governing community in which residents are involved in decision-making was another over-arching aim.

Vision

Ebbsfleet Garden City is the first in a new generation of large-scale, locally led planned communities, and as such has developed a vision which continues the tradition of great place-making in the UK; combining the best of urban and rural living, and building on the ethos and pioneering spirit of Georgian, Victorian and Edwardian planned communities to define a benchmark for 21st century development.

Key details

- A 20-year, city-scale proposal for 15,000 new homes, and up to 32,000 additional jobs, supported by appropriate infrastructure and community facilities, together with the potential for a world-class theme park at Swanscombe Peninsula.

- Located in north Kent, 'where London meets the Garden of England', based around the High-Speed 1 rail hub at Ebbsfleet International Station, the development embraces the existing communities of Swanscombe and Greenhithe, and is sandwiched between the River Thames to the north and the Kent countryside to the south.

- Led by the Healthy New Town (HNT) Partnership; NHS England; Ebbsfleet Development Corporation (EDC); Dartford, Gravesham and Swanley Clinical Commissioning Group; with significant support from Kent County Council.

- Staged targets include 5,100 new homes and a 10% improvement in *Quality of Life Indices* by 2021, with the completed garden city vision realised by 2035.

- A wide range of housing opportunities for everyone: 30% (4,500) of new homes to be affordable, and a further 5% (250) specialist homes for older or vulnerable groups, to be completed by 2021.

Objectives

The programme aims to improve the health outcomes and health benefits of communities living in designated HNTs by considering an innovative approach to the design of the place and the health services provided, from the outset. There is an opportunity to understand and re-establish the relationship between health and housing quality, including the design of homes, streets and neighbourhoods, including their potential impact on how people can live healthier and happier lives. This concept was central to the theory behind early New Towns and Garden Cities.

The HNT Programme for Ebbsfleet Garden City has been developed around three work streams – 'Built Environment', 'Community Building' and developing new 'Models of Care' – recognising that we must consider holistically where people live, how they live and interact, and how they can access services and facilities.

The HNT partners aim to achieve a number of key outcomes including creating an active and vibrant city, delivering an accessible blue and green infrastructure, and allowing people to live independently at home for longer.

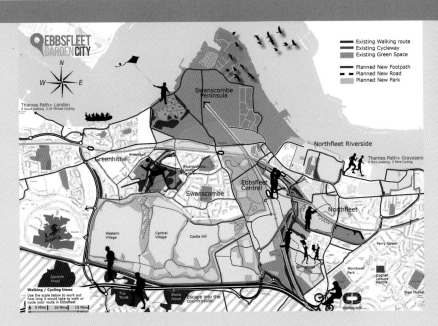

Legend:
Existing Walking route
Existing Cycleway
Existing Green Space
Planned New Footpath
Planned New Road
Planned New Park

← ← The new Health, Innovation and Education Quarter.

← Walking and cycling map.

There are intentions to:

- Define the principles of a 'Healthy Garden City for everyone'.

- Promote particular design and sustainability features (flexible layouts, renewable technology) and areas of innovation (community hub, mixed tenure, use of assistive technology, care provision, unusual procurement route).

- Embed the principles of good place-making, promote best practice in the design of homes and public buildings, and consider long-term stewardship from the outset.

- Develop an Ebbsfleet Garden City 'Quality Mark' to set a benchmark for design quality.

- Realise the ambition through the HNT Partnership, and transfer lessons to other HNT pilot sites.

Built environment workstream

The focus of this workstream is to combine the existing, natural features of the location with new physical interventions to help encourage positive interactions between residents and their environment. This should promote healthier and more active lifestyles through the design of homes, streets and neighbourhoods, which support independent living for longer. It encompasses three key projects:

1 A Quality Marking: A voluntary checklist to be used by developers, consultants, EDC staff, and future residents and workers to help determine what 'good practice' means for a 21st century Healthy Garden City. (To be produced by Design for Homes, drawing on their HAPPI experience).

2 A Health, Education and Innovation Quarter: To include a health and well-being hub, specialist housing for older people with access to health services, research, diagnostic, education and innovation facilities, and housing for health workers. (Key concepts to be developed by Sarah Wigglesworth Architects, embedding learning from the DWELL project) (see pp 100–105).

3 A Landscape Design Challenge: To explore how the design of landscape, and positive engagement with it, can help stimulate better health outcomes for everyone, with a specific focus on an ageing population. (To be undertaken by the HNT Team working with the Landscape Institute, using the findings to inform the design of seven new city parks).

Recognising that there is value in 'healthy homes in a healthy city' for developers and consumers, the HNT will use the outputs when working collaboratively with developers and consultants to achieve good design. The programme aims to be 'radical but realisable' – promote fresh ideas, offer professional support when needed and signpost good practice when appropriate.

Kevin McGeough, Director of Ebbsfleet Garden City, Healthy New Town and Head of Placemaking, Ebbsfleet Development Corporation.

SUBURBAN INTENSIFICATION

The general approach to the design and density of suburban housing has barely changed over the last 40 years. Across the country, new suburban development still comprises a mix of detached and semi-detached houses, often with a few short runs of terraced houses and perhaps a three or four storey block of walk-up flats, rarely exceeding 35 dwellings per hectare.

Lifetime Homes has been patchily applied and many new suburban houses are not suitable for older people – largely because it has been too easy to market and sell to first-time buyers and young families. Few have contained any purpose-built retirement housing either. The Home Builders Federation (HBF) and enlightened individual developers are beginning to recognise that older people are a potentially lucrative market. The Women's Royal Voluntary Service (WRVS) estimates that the future value of older people's spending power will have grown to £127 billion by 2030 (including multiplier effects), representing growth of around 68% over 2010 levels.[56]

In 2014, Barratt Homes launched a downsizer range and other volume house-builders are following suit. Tony Pidgley CBE, Chair of Berkeley Group Holdings PLC, reported to the All Party Parliamentary Group (APPG) inquiry into Housing and Care for Older People that, the downsizer product is now their second biggest market.[57]

Politicians are recognising that downsizing and using land more efficiently are essential ways to tackle the housing crisis. New, low-maintenance homes with fewer (but larger) rooms, and small gardens or roof terraces are the obvious answer for many of the older people who are not averse to moving but prefer to remain in mainstream housing. Courtyard houses can achieve densities of 60–75 dwellings per hectare and while a small garden represents a significant compromise for most families, it can be a relief for many older people. *Designing with Downsizers*, part of the DWELL project, reinforces this (see p 100 and pp102–105).[58]

> ❝ …the future value of older people's spending power will have grown to £127 billion by 2030 (including multiplier effects), representing growth of around 68% over 2010 levels.

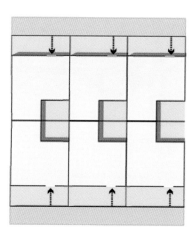

↑ The plot efficiency is evident when the houses are grouped.

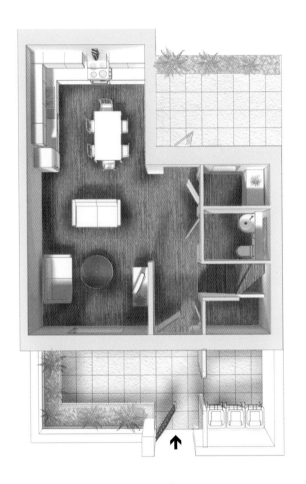

← Generic example of efficient, tightly grouped, two storey courtyard housing.

Ground floor plan

First floor plan

↑ Homely, suburban
scale achieved at Heald
Farm Court extra care
development (Case Study 8).

2.3 The importance of a good brief

SETTING CLEAR GOALS

Briefing is often an informal and iterative process. Where specialised housing is envisaged, the wide range of options and the significant management and operational implications make a reasonably clear and comprehensive initial brief particularly important. The design concept must be informed by an understanding of the client's overarching aims, the likely resident/customer group, the way in which care and support are to be delivered, the degree of public access and the budget, as well as the site and its surroundings.

Maximising dwelling numbers and efficient spatial planning tend to be priorities in all housing projects. In extra care schemes the general view of most providers has been that at least 50–60 flats are needed to cover the cost of the additional facilities, make on-site catering viable and keep service charges manageable. A combination of reducing subsidy and rising land cost is tending to lead to larger developments.

Taken together, communal facilities and circulation spaces often represent at least 35% of the total internal floor area; almost double the 20% expected of a mainstream apartment block. The client should therefore provide a schedule of the size and type of communal spaces, administration areas and ancillary spaces that are required. Underestimating the extent and cost of supporting space often leads to an overestimate of the number of homes that can be achieved, causing viability problems further down the line.

Those who commission housing for people with high care needs often expect a single building, or at least for all spaces used by residents to be connected by a covered route. This inevitably generates a large footprint, a tall building, or both. How scale and articulation are handled is crucial to successful physical integration, particularly in low-rise suburban or rural settings. The need for step-free access adds to the challenge of a large footprint on sloping sites, but this too, can be turned into an asset through careful design. Many schemes manage these challenges positively.

MANAGEMENT AND MAINTENANCE

Designers must start with a basic understanding of how the completed development will be managed. Decisions begin at the front entrance and permeate throughout – inside and out. In particular, the concept of progressive privacy (see pp 63–64) will inform the layout of the building and the way in which access, security, means of escape, and care delivery are resolved. It will affect how the building works and feels, particularly how homely it feels. The extent to which the facilities will be open to the public is also a major factor.

Strategies will need to be confirmed in areas such as catering, deliveries, assistive technology, fire safety, energy, metering and waste management. It may be some time before these issues are fully resolved, but early discussion saves time and improves built outcomes.

Facilitating maintenance and reducing disruption are high priorities in buildings that are continuously occupied and intensively used by vulnerable people. While it is important to offer residents control over the environmental conditions within their homes, in managed buildings it is preferable to install as much heating and ventilation equipment as possible out of apartments and into circulation areas to facilitate maintenance. Subject to fire safety requirements, service risers and cupboards should be in discreet but accessible locations with tamperproof locks to prevent vulnerable residents becoming confused or harmed. Overhead pipework in corridors should be lagged to mitigate overheating (see p 86).

---

i INFO │ Checklist of items to be confirmed in an individual project brief

1. Overall targets

- Number of apartments
- Number of residents (based on estimate of singles and couples)
- Number of parking spaces (with breakdown for residents, visitors and staff)
- Number of cycle spaces (with breakdown for residents, visitors and staff).

2. Resident group

- Age range
- Tenure
- Lifestyle requirements
- Care needs
- Special needs (dementia, cultural requirements etc)
- Respite care and/or 'step up' or 'step down care' following a stay in hospital.

3. Brief for communal spaces

- Dining space (size, preferred arrangement, whether servery required)
- Lounge/sitting areas (size, number, distribution)
- Assisted bathrooms/treatment rooms (number, distribution)

- Guest suites (number, distribution)
- Any additional facilities required including:
    - Residents' tea/snack room
    - Quiet room/library
    - IT suite
    - Gym/fitness suite
    - Swimming pool
    - Public access (which, if any, facilities to be open to the public).

4. Brief for apartments

- Tenure split (number of apartments for each tenure)
- Dwelling mix (breakdown by tenure)
- Dwelling type (number of wheelchair adaptable and accessible apartments, by mix and tenure)
- Target floor areas
- Special or additional requirements including preferences for:
    - Open plan layout/separate rooms
    - Bathroom access (whether en suite required)
    - Showers/baths (which to install at the outset)

    - Additional WCs/bathrooms
    - Built-in wardrobes
    - Balconies or winter gardens.

5. Strategies to be developed in the early stages of the project

- Access and security
- Reception requirements and mail delivery
- Mobility scooter, wheelchair and cycle storage
- Fire protection and means of escape
- Technology and communications
- Catering
- Waste management (whether holding points are needed on each floor)
- Metering arrangements (whether homes are individually metered or costs shared)
- Energy and CO_2 reduction
- SuDS, biodiversity and ecology
- Maintenance of indoor and outdoor space.

6. Confirmation of the Planning Use Class, local planning standards and regulations

2.4 Option appraisal and design concept

GETTING THE DIAGRAM RIGHT

The early stages of a project seek to test a range of options at an increasing level of detail. The process is iterative rather than linear; through diagrams, drawings, precedents and dialogue, the aim is to find the solution that best responds to the brief and the site. Concept drawings should concentrate on the basic form, massing, layout and orientation of the building (or buildings), how it relates to its immediate surroundings, where it will be entered, and where the principal indoor and outdoor spaces will be located.

From the start, designers need to consider the daily experience of the future occupants. As we age, we spend more time at home and are less able to adjust to fluctuating internal environmental conditions (see pp 85–86). Being less mobile makes the view out of the window from our favourite chair, the ease with which we can take a shower, open a window or get out onto our balcony, all the more important. Research conducted by the University of York provides valuable pointers for design.[59]

LOCATING ENTRANCES AND KEY SPACES

A single entrance for residents and visitors allows for easier control and therefore greater security – a particularly important consideration when designing for people with dementia or reduced capacity. Staff will often use the main entrance too. Even where a manned reception desk is envisaged, it is usually desirable to have a second layer of security (an inner door with fobbed access) between the entrance area and any parts of the building containing private apartments, as there will always be times when the receptionist is busy or away from the desk.

Secondary 'residential entrances' offer a more private way home and work particularly well for more independent residents, but the security implications should be discussed. As a general rule, the main social spaces (typically shared lounges and dining rooms) should be close to the main entrance, as should any areas that are open to the public (see p 63).

The location of the kitchen is often the most challenging issue to resolve. It needs to serve the most prominent spaces (lounge and dining areas) but adjoin the least attractive (cold store, refuse area and service yard). Generic guidance is difficult; some clients require a large, single kitchen to serve separate eating areas for the public and residents (and yet remain unobtrusive) while others choose smaller, dispersed cooking areas as a more homely, and more sociable, option (see pp 62–63). It is essential to have these discussions early.

REMEMBERING OTHER USERS

Care and support staff, and those working in management, administration, catering and cleaning, all need quiet spaces for respite and relaxation in addition to well-equipped, functional work places. The design should actively encourage visitors by creating spaces that people want to spend time in. All ages need to be considered; visits, for instance, are often cut short because children have become bored so it is important to consider incidental play opportunities in easily supervised indoor and outdoor areas (see p 63 for guest suites).

→ Residents enjoy the company of young visitors in Faelledgaarden Retirement Home.

← A light and comfortable space for staff to relax and talk in the same development.

LIVING ACCOMMODATION FOR PARTNERS

Confronting the reality that you or your partner needs, or is likely to need, significantly more care than the other is able to provide, can be extremely distressing. Homecare is an option but is not always practical, available or affordable. Extra care and retirement housing schemes typically offer a number of apartments with two or more bedrooms, which are suitable for couples, and many are able to meet high care needs. But while moving together may seem like the obvious answer, there are practical and financial implications to consider. Currently, when one partner remains at home, the value of the home is not counted in the means testing that determines who pays for social care.

The separate, on-site accommodation offered at Gradmann Haus (see p 17) for the partners and spouses of its residents, allows couples to spend as much time together as they wish, without the burden of one being the full-time carer. It is not without complication (what happens when the partner with dementia dies or the other begins to need care themselves?) but the humanity of this concept makes it an important model for the future, particularly in specialised facilities for people living with dementia. Lodge Road, in St. John's Wood, London (Case Study 12) offers similar opportunities.

RESPITE, POST-HOSPITAL AND END-OF-LIFE CARE

Some developments offer short-term respite care and/or 'step up' or 'step down' facilities to support people to regain their independence following a short stay in hospital, and this will have an impact on design and management. Hospices also play an extremely important role in respite and end-of-life care.

EXAMPLE | Urban Hospice and end of life care, Copenhagen

NORD Architects has created a modern hospice in the heart of Frederiksberg, an historic and densely populated district of Copenhagen. The building, which fronts a busy street, is seen as a community asset; it is designed to be inclusive and welcoming while offering privacy, dignity and palliative care to people whose lives are ending.

Providing 16 beds and a number of shared spaces, it is conceived as a 'house', not an institution. The traditional corridor is broken down into smaller sections, the inside is hollowed out to enclose a private inner courtyard and the external materials are warm and tactile. The result of a collaborative process, it aims to provide 'a good place to die'.

Guinness Care and Support has an extensive portfolio of sheltered housing schemes that are in need of considerable updating or redevelopment. To help assess the best way forward for each development the trust has developed a set of benchmark standards, based on the ten HAPPI principles (see p 18). Using the benchmark, Wimshurst Pelleriti has produced a number of options to upgrade an existing facility in Havant. The addition of an extra floor may prove crucial to financial viability.

2.5 Working with existing buildings

REMODELLING EXISTING FACILITIES

Much of the sheltered housing built over the last 50 years is now in need of replacement. Those facilities that can be saved usually need substantial repair and/or remodelling. General expectations have risen as these buildings have become tired; apartments have tended to increase in size, and private balconies, high thermal and acoustic performance, and good daylight are routinely expected, making upgrading a significant challenge. Typical shortcomings include:

- Very small flats
- No provision for mobility scooters
- Poor insulation, and issues of fuel poverty
- Shortage or absence of lifts
- Steps
- Shared bathrooms
- Limited access to poor quality external spaces
- Long, dark and unfriendly corridors
- Poor natural light
- Limited potential for assistive technology.

While a presumption in favour of retention is a responsible starting point, it is important to remain open-minded and test the extent to which the building is capable of satisfying current expectations. It will usually be sensible to explore, and cost, a range of options, including the potential to add an extension, or replace part, or all, of the building and integrate technology. The deciding factor will often be the scope to increase scale and density, and where the existing facility has to remain operational, this will be a significant constraint. Many older care homes also need substantial modernisation.

CONVERSIONS INVOLVING CHANGE OF USE

The same principles apply to conversions involving change of use. While it is important to retain and repurpose high quality buildings with character and presence, and in good locations, they need to work. Meeting the practical demands of a brief for specialised housing in a non-residential building may be challenging, particularly if the building is listed. It may be more appropriate to convert the retained buildings to communal spaces, which tend to be more flexible than apartments. Willow Barns (Case Study 9) incorporates and converts an existing barn to provide communal facilities and a plant room.

EXAMPLE | One Bayshill, Cheltenham, Gloucestershire

Working for PegasusLife, Glenn Howells Architects (GHA) is transforming two pairs of Grade II listed Georgian villas into 48 retirement living apartments with shared facilities including a hydrotherapy spa, lounge and restaurant. Situated in a prominent location, the villas had been clumsily combined into a single property. GHA has replaced the insensitive additions with a new element that allows the original villa forms to be read, and acknowledges their neoclassical proportions. An ugly mansard has been removed and the villas' garden setting and railings reinstated. The new middle section is subservient to the scale and massing of the villas and is clad in Bath stone to respond to prominent nearby buildings such as Cheltenham Ladies' College.

BESPOKE ADAPTATIONS

At the other end of the scale, bespoke adaptations or extensions to individual homes can make an enormous difference to an older person's quality of life. A means-tested Disability Facilities Grant (DFG) may be available from local authorities, but is currently capped at £30,000. Work will often involve a housing association or private landlord, and an occupational therapist and/or carer, as well as the individual and their family. It is important not to underestimate the time the project may take.

← Gentle encouragement can make all the difference, (Case Study 15).

INSIGHT | The role of occupational therapists

Occupational therapists work with people who may have a combination of physical, sensory, cognitive and neuro-diverse impairments, many of which are more common in older people. The aim is to help people to live life the way they choose.

Taking a person-centred approach, they play a crucial role in ensuring that an individual's home is as safe and accessible as possible. Working closely with the people concerned, this often involves identifying specialist equipment, and/or making recommendations for the design of bespoke adaptations. This

may mean creating level or ramped access (in place of steps), installing a level access shower, wheelchair accessible kitchen, stair-lift, through-floor lift or ceiling hoist. It often involves close cooperation with building professionals who have the technical expertise to deliver the most practical solutions.

A growing number of occupational therapists are also using their specialist skills and experience to contribute to the design and construction of new accessible and inclusive housing, particularly homes intended for wheelchair users. Where the

end user is not known, the challenge is to design a home that will work for most people, while avoiding over-specification and undue cost. Close collaboration with architects, designers and developers at the outset is key to delivering this objective.

Marney Walker, independent occupational therapist and specialist in accessible home design.

Jacquel Runnalls, independent occupational therapist specialising in accessible and inclusive design and a Senior Occupational Therapist in Housing for a London borough.

2.6 Summary

A great deal of work takes place before the design team is even appointed. The decision to proceed will be informed by the client's previous experience, aims, ethos and budget, an assessment of demand/need, the site location and the character of the area. Even when the type of facility has been decided there are relatively few hard and fast rules, but it is possible to identify a number of issues that will always warrant careful, often open-minded, consideration.

Inevitably, the initial residents of any development will age and the concept of a 'home for life' increases the range of age, need and support that must be accommodated. Clients and designers must work through the complexities implied by this, and commit to solutions that will work now and over time. Early dialogue is essential and, as is often the case, success lies in the holistic resolution of a wide range of practical and logistical challenges. A failure in just one area can compromise the whole.

In some parts of buildings, the impact of good design is overt – immediately apparent, often impressive; in others, its role is deliberately covert – intended to facilitate smooth running behind the scenes and allow systems to work invisibly. This dichotomy often becomes more relevant in highly specialised environments for more vulnerable people in order that they can continue to enjoy relative independence with appropriate support.

3.0 The social value of shared space

This chapter applies largely to specialised housing. It looks at the important role that shared indoor and outdoor spaces play in alleviating loneliness and promoting healthy lifestyles, and it investigates the use of design to encourage social interaction and develop a sense of community while respecting privacy and independence.

'Soloinsieme', the invented term that combines the Italian words for 'alone' and 'together', sums up what many regard as the best of both worlds: independent living accommodation with shared spaces that bring people together and offer easy opportunities to enjoy a change of scene without the need to travel – one of the main reasons why those who opt to move to 'group settings' make that choice. While some spaces are specifically designed with sociability in mind, others simply encourage incidental, neighbourly encounters.

↑ A dynamic atrium provides
a visual connnection between
multiple floors at Limelight
extra care housing, Trafford,
Greater Manchester (PRP for
Trafford Housing Trust).

❝ **Buildings cannot
force us to be
sociable but they
can encourage social
interaction.**

3.1 Encouraging social interaction through form and layout

MORE THAN A CORRIDOR

Buildings cannot force us to be sociable but they can encourage social interaction. Even a diagrammatic layout gives clues about the sociability of the ultimate development. Entrance and circulation areas are often the places where incidental encounters and unplanned conversations take place. For too long, the default option has been long, internal corridors with apartments on both sides; efficient, but institutional, they rarely become inviting places to linger.

Wide, covered access decks are possibly the most sociable alternative, particularly when they are wide enough for sitting out. Many people enjoy having to 'go out' to use the dining room or lounge but as this can be an issue for frailer residents, partial protection (ideally sliding screens or windows) should be considered. Naturally lit, single-sided corridors or atria are good 'indoor' alternatives. An atrium allows residents on upper floors to feel more connected, and aids legibility but often requires a 'drop-down curtain' to prevent the spread of fire. Guidance from the National Fire Chiefs Council (NFCC) may be helpful and specialist advice should be sought early.[60]

Whichever form of circulation is employed, shallow, recessed entrances to individual apartments work well. As well as visually breaking up the corridor or deck, this increases opportunities for personalisation and conversation. Coupled with small, fixed windows (typically from apartment kitchens and subject to

← Open decks and cloistered arrangements promote social interaction at Pilgrim Gardens, Evington, Leicester. (PRP for Pilgrims' Friend Society).

fire safety approval) these simple moves can turn a corridor into a 'street' and aid wayfinding.

Commenting on feedback from residents of Rochdale Boroughwide Housing's Hare Hill, an extra care scheme in Littleborough, Damian Utton of Pozzoni architects noted that:

The kitchen windows looking onto the corridor areas are popular. Some residents have taken the opportunity to personalise these windows in various creative ways. Residents have also commented that these windows give them reassurance that they are not alone.

COURTYARD LAYOUTS

Courtyard or quadrangle arrangements tend to predominate in extra care schemes. This is understandable and generally practical. Most clients prefer to offer every resident access to at least two lifts to provide cover in the event of breakdown or during routine maintenance, and a looped arrangement (a continuous corridor) facilitates this. Offering at least two choices of direction for access and egress (including means of escape), it also reduces the need for escape stairs.

While a loop will always bring you back to your starting point and avoids the dead ends that can be particularly disconcerting for people living with dementia, there is an alternative view that it can cause some residents (again often those living with dementia) to tire and become dehydrated by 'endless walking'. The preferred solution may depend partly on staffing levels.

By their nature, courtyards are protected, semi-private, calm, static spaces that imply collective access and ownership. The Oxbridge quadrangles, and most early monasteries, are familiar examples. If there is a drawback, it is that these spaces can feel introspective, even institutional; but much depends on the scale, the surrounding uses and how the circulation is handled. In traditional models the courtyard is lined with a cloister. As contemporary buildings tend to be taller, all-round multilayered decks or corridors can start to feel oppressive. Care also needs to be taken to protect privacy within apartments that face into a courtyard.

3.2 Creating spaces that people want to use

COMING TOGETHER

For a great many people, communal areas are not just a way of avoiding loneliness; they are a positive opportunity to socialise, take part in activities or be entertained. Almost all developments provide at least one communal lounge area, a communal dining room and a shared outdoor space. Many also offer a range of other activity, learning and therapeutic spaces, including a library, IT suite, hobbies room, gym or exercise room and a spa. Retirement villages often go further still – providing workspace, shops, cashpoints, a bar, cinema and/or a swimming pool.

The location and inter-location of key spaces, their proportion, outlook, quality of light, materials,

> ... on the whole, well-designed spaces become well-used and well-loved.

acoustics and many other factors affect the extent to which they encourage social interaction. As individuals we respond according to our mood and preferences: different spaces may appeal at different times of day, or in different seasons. Our reactions are usually instinctive; on the whole, well-designed spaces become well-used and well-loved.

LARGE MULTIPURPOSE SPACES

Lounge and dining areas are conventionally seen as the most sociable spaces but it can be difficult to avoid an institutional feel, particularly in larger developments. Providers often require a space that is large enough for 60–75 people to eat together (typically 110–120m^2 excluding storage) and though there are effective ways to subdivide such spaces, these tend to restrict their ability to accommodate other functions, such as exercise, events or performances.

The flexibility of a fully multifunctional space has to be weighed against the risk that it does nothing very well. Advances in product and system design, for elements such as lighting, moveable walls and blackout facilities, have helped but it is still important to focus on the primary, or most frequent use. Where this is dining, the space will need a reasonably hard, non-slip, washable floor finish; good views; high levels of natural light; flexible, dimmable, artificial lighting and some acoustic treatment on the walls and/or the ceiling to keep noise to a manageable level.

The room will need to connect to the kitchen (typically via a servery) and often a bar. It should have a discrete space for coats and wheelchairs, and be within easy reach of accessible WCs. All of this will be necessary to support events too. Without the tables, a room of 110–120m^2 could provide auditorium-style seating for an audience of approximately 100. Between meals, tables can be rearranged to create a space for craftwork, cooking, exercise, Pilates, yoga or dance. Though shifting furniture inevitably causes some noise and disruption, it also generates activity, changes the feel of the space and can create a sense of purpose and anticipation. Large rooms need a correspondingly generous floor to ceiling height. Where accommodation is placed above, care must be taken to avoid half levels and ramps. Managing drainage from bathrooms and kitchens above can also be a challenge. While a column-free space offers the most flexibility, transfer structures are expensive.

← Residents enjoy a game of pool in the main lounge of Hoergaarden Retirement Home, Copenhagen.

↓ The multi-functional, ground floor hub at Limelight is open to the public.

↑ Residents meeting over tea in the 'common house' of New Ground (Case Study 4).

SOCIABLE SITTING SPACES

The main dining/function room is much less likely to double as a comfortable sitting space: partly due to its size and ambience, and partly because moving armchairs and sofas on a daily basis is impractical. Dedicated lounge areas tend to work better, but they too, are often oversized and can feel like a hotel foyer.

The idea that older people need privacy and must look out onto a quiet space that is not overlooked is another commonly held misconception. In truth, while some do, others prefer closer contact with the wider community – the opportunity to watch children walking home from school, dustbins being collected, hedges being trimmed – life being lived. Time passes more quickly when things are going on and it helps to reduce loneliness.

↑ Residents of De Hogeweyk are encouraged to help with meal preparation, (Case Study 15).

Choice is therefore important. Rather than one large lounge, it may be preferable to provide two or more smaller sitting areas, each with a different feel and outlook. It often works well to locate one in, or close to, the entrance lobby where the daily coming and going of staff, visitors and deliveries provides interest in itself; and another linked to a small kitchen for tea and snack-making, or adjoining a bar. Ideally, each should connect to a different type of outdoor space. As noted in the previous chapter (see p 49) an increasing number of developments are being arranged into 'households', each with shared spaces of a more domestic scale. In Ørestad (Case Study 13), flexible sitting/eating/cooking spaces are dispersed on all floors, and residents are encouraged to participate in food preparation and cooking.

FUNCTIONAL AND THERAPEUTIC SPACES

Other spaces and facilities vary considerably from project to project. The size of the development, what already exists nearby, and the extent to which the proposed facilities will be open to the wider public, are key factors.

Extra care developments usually provide a hairdressing service and at least one assisted bathroom. The former should feel like a professional salon and will be an important social space. It may include a couch for therapy, beauty treatment and massage. Assisted bathrooms are also increasingly seen as therapeutic environments rather than clinical spaces. Soft lighting, relaxing music, warm colours and sleek, contemporary fittings promote dignity and wellbeing. It may be appropriate to combine an assisted bathroom and hairdressing salon into a multifunctional 'spa' or 'wellness space'. A gym or fitness suite and a range of other activity spaces are also typically provided in large developments.

GUEST SUITES

Friends and relatives often travel long distances to visit older people who may tire easily, perhaps taking an afternoon nap. Waking up to visitors can be confusing, and discovering that they have to leave soon, disappointing. Overnight guest accommodation can make the experience more positive and less stressful for everyone. A guest suite usually comprises a large wheelchair accessible bedroom, with twin beds, tea-making facilities and an en suite shower (similar to a good quality hotel bedroom). When space allows, a small apartment with extra pull-out beds is useful for families.

3.3 Progressive privacy

Progressive privacy provides a framework for determining where different spaces need to be located and how they should be accessed. It guides the planning and zoning of buildings that combine private, shared and public or semi-public spaces. The aim is to ensure that different types of users have convenient and intuitive access to the parts of the building that are intended for them, but are steered away from (and unable to access) other parts.

In broad terms, the more privacy required, the deeper and/or higher into the scheme the facility should be, and the greater the security. By implication, the most public facilities should be closest to the main entrance, usually on the same floor level. In addition to the user groups listed above, some staff will need access to all parts of the building, others to specific areas only. There will also be areas designated for staff use only.

Notwithstanding the importance of security and progressive privacy, the building should feel open, accessible and sociable, and be easy to navigate – avoiding dead-ends and anonymous corridors, and encouraging the incidental encounters that are so valuable. The principles of progressive privacy and security should be applied to external spaces too.

3.4 Access to care and support

CARE-READY ENVIRONMENTS

One of the defining characteristics of age-friendly housing is that it is 'care-ready': able to facilitate person-delivered care and accommodate assistive technology. Specialised 'group housing' offers economies of scale and allows personal care to be delivered more efficiently due to reduced travel time and a purpose-built environment. This not only makes sophisticated technology more affordable, it also makes it feel more normal. There are generally three elements to a care-ready environment:

- **Physical characteristics:** Indoor and outdoor spaces that are designed and built to eliminate barriers, accommodate wheelchairs, accept aids and lifting devices and facilitate independence in themselves.
- **Person-centred care:** Places and management arrangements that support the delivery of personalised care, and the carers themselves (whether partners, friends, relatives or paid professionals).
- **Smart and assistive technology:** Technology-enabled environments that incorporate, or could incorporate, digital/smart devices, such as telecare and assistive technology, and facilitate its use and management.

Technology is the area likely to undergo the most change. The digital revolution is affecting every aspect of daily life and has enormous potential to further improve the lives of older people. Already,

← Care and support can encompass a range of therapies and treatments including podiatry and massage.

the possibilities range from various sensors and alarms (a neck pendant being the simplest) to highly sophisticated monitoring devices and robotic companions or carers.

Phone alerts can remind people with dementia to drink or eat, take medication or go for a walk. Personalised monitoring devices are now able to detect what is 'normal for us', and by implication, what is 'not normal for us'. Special contact lenses can test and monitor blood sugar levels, and cameras can record the subtle changes in posture that suggest a person may be likely to experience a fall, or a stroke, 48 hours later.

The increasing role of technology in care delivery must be part of a wider ethical debate about the extent to which machines, including robots, should replace human contact, who should have access to personal data, and what happens when technology fails. Used wisely it can increase social connectivity, not diminish it. These themes are explored in more detail in Chapter 5.0 and Case Study 5.

COMMUNITY HUBS

Many extra care schemes and retirement villages offer some sort of hub; typically for use by residents and their visitors but open to the public at certain times. These, and other stand-alone hubs, such as that planned at Ebbsfleet (see pp 42–43) could play a significantly wider role in communities – supporting older people living independently and offering a range of services and facilities to people of all ages. Urban Hospice (see p 51) fulfils some of the same functions.

🗨 VIEWPOINT | The potential of community care hubs and 'HAPPI housing'

A community care hub can play a key role in meeting the housing, care and support needs for older people within their own neighbourhoods. A hub is flexible in concept, configuration, and the services and/or accommodation it offers. It can operate on a single site or be part of a network of specialist housing options, services and facilities distributed around a neighbourhood or town:

- **Community facilities:** A hub might include a range of facilities for the surrounding community such as a crèche, healthy-living centre, library, adult education facilities, a community hall, gym and health club and so on.

- **Care and support services:** It could include a community resource centre (with information on care and support services for the local community), a base for homecare providers operating in the area, services offering day care, meals on wheels, laundry, transport, a handyman service (for aids and adaptations to homes in the community) and so on.

- **Health services:** Health facilities such as a GP surgery, community based healthcare centre, re-enablement or 'step down' facility, or healthy-living centre could also be included.

- **Housing:** A hub might also include a range of residential accommodation offering short-term and/or longer tenure options such as rehabilitation, respite care, dementia care, extra care or inclusively designed 'HAPPI housing', strategically located, to share the communal and health facilities.

- **Location specific:** It can be tailored to the particular needs of a community in terms of the facilities and services that it provides. This will require close coordination and collaboration between key stakeholders such as local authority housing, adult services, local care providers, clinical commissioning groups, community interest groups, residents and the developer in order to develop the brief and agree revenue funding arrangements.

- **Integrated:** It must be 'integrated' within the fabric of the community by virtue of the range of services and facilities it offers, its location and its design, which should be 'contextual' and 'welcoming'. Its facilities should present an open and attractive 'shopfront' to the community.

- **Technology:** The employment of assistive technology, telecare and telehealth will play an increasingly important role in communication, underpinning community-based care networks as a more tech-savvy generation approaches an age where it will require care and support.

If widely adopted by local authorities as a community-based concept for supporting and caring for their ageing populations, the combination of community hubs and inclusively designed housing could provide a sound and sustainable solution for one of the greatest challenges facing our society.

Roger Battersby, former managing partner, PRP architects and HAPPI expert panellist.

3.5 Convivial outdoor spaces

REINFORCING CONNECTIONS

Although we tend to spend less time outside as we get older, we value the external environment just as much – and at all scales. People often say that the natural world becomes more important with age; that there is more time to appreciate the small things, such as bird song and nest-building, as well as to reflect on the bigger issues of climate change and environmental sustainability. We often transfer a great deal of hope and expectation to our children and grandchildren, and the changing seasons can be a comforting reminder that cyclical decline and renewal is natural and inevitable.

In practice, our physical world – the space we regularly access and use – shrinks as we become frailer. That makes it all the more important to make it as rich and stimulating as possible, through the course of each day, and the year as a whole. We know too, that exposure to sunlight facilitates the production of vitamin D, which increases bone strength and muscle performance, resulting in fewer and less severe falls. When external spaces are treated as an extension

⬇ Convivial, enclosed, outdoor space at Pilgrim Gardens.

➜ Croquet lawn, accesible from the lounge area at St Bede's, Bedford. (PRP for Orbit Group).

to a popular internal space, they are better used. Visual access is as important as physical access; large windows with low cills bring the outside in, and open up a space. Recent evidence suggests that simply being able to see a tree from our home has a positive impact on wellbeing.[61]

SCALE AND CHARACTER

Many of the factors that determine the success of indoor spaces – size, shape, orientation, character and a focal point – apply equally to outdoor spaces. Here too, choice is important. A courtyard feels very different from the more amorphous space around the edge of a building. The latter can be a rather difficult 'no-man's land', particularly when it abuts ground floor

apartments. Often mediating between private and semi-private, it should be full of seasonal interest and easy to manage. Depending on the depth of the space and the resident group, it can provide a pleasant, meandering walking route, interspersed with frequent resting points and possibly a gentle fitness trail with informal exercise equipment.

Courtyards can often be treated as outdoor rooms with all-weather furnishing. They should offer a choice of sun and shade, seasonal interest and space for shared activities. Good lighting extends the hours of interest, can provide dramatic impact, and is vital for safety. A sculpture or specimen tree can become a well-loved focal point. Easy access to a WC is also important.

↑ Intimate courtyard at
Hazelhurst Court, Lewisham,
London. (Levitt Bernstein
for Phoenix Community
Housing Association).

↑ Rooftop walkway
and amenity space at
Halton Court, Kidbrooke,
Greenwich. (PRP for Berkeley
Homes Urban Renaissance).

PLANTING AND WILDLIFE

Trees and plants are the most obvious indicators of the seasons as well as the main source of outdoor colour and texture. Many plants are also fragrant, tactile or edible, sometimes all three. Rarely static, they attract and provide habitats for insects, birds and small mammals. The choice of planting is important; while evergreens provide consistent colour, they offer less year-round interest and the fresh spring growth of herbaceous perennials is uniquely optimistic.

Larger developments often include a kitchen garden. Fresh produce is particularly beneficial to older people because our ability to metabolise vitamins and minerals, and our sense of taste, both tend to reduce with age. Gardening generally, and food growing in particular, is immensely satisfying and often very social. While digging may have to be left to the most active, almost everyone can participate in watering, weeding and harvesting, particularly when raised beds are used. These activities, and the colour, texture and smell of fruit and vegetables, often evoke positive and reassuring memories especially for people living with dementia, and can bring a sense of achievement too. Simple rituals such as hanging out washing or feeding chickens have similarly beneficial effects on memory and wellbeing.

EXAMPLE | Shared garden maintained by residents

Joan, an 81-year-old resident of Bredon Almshouses, helps the gardener to maintain its delightful courtyard garden. Joan loves plants and is determined to stay active. Together, they have planned and planted the borders and the terrace using colourful, cottage perennials that complement the character and scale of the 17th century building, bring pleasure and pride to the other residents and contribute to the village as a whole.

ℹ INFO | HenPower

The therapeutic effects of hen-keeping led to the setting up of HenPower, an organisation that describes itself as 'a leading creative ageing charity supporting older people and those living with dementia in Gateshead, Newcastle and across the UK'. Now active in more than 40 care homes, HenPower engages older people in arts activities and hen-keeping to promote health and wellbeing and reduce loneliness.

Next to blindness, loneliness is the worst thing you can have, it is a big affliction. It can destroy a lot of people. I know because I have been through it. At 87, hens are the biggest thing in our lives. [62]

Ossie Cresswell, HenPower enthusiast

↑ The formal pond is a
focal point in the landscape
of Pilgrim Gardens.

WATER

Moving water plays with light and generates sound and movement. Often soothing and sometimes mesmerising, the presence of water can be particularly helpful for people experiencing dementia. Even small ponds, narrow rills and simple spouts introduce a dynamic quality to a space and attract wildlife that would not otherwise be present.

Water can also be used in practical ways, such as swales and ponds forming part of a sustainable urban drainage system (SuDS). As with all external elements, water must be always be introduced safely and in a controlled way. Poor design, specification or construction of outdoor spaces can result in serious hazards; every detail needs to be extremely carefully considered.

socialise and eat together, creates a more homely environment with greater opportunities for participation but will have implications for staffing levels. Location, proportion, good views, sunlight, good natural and artificial light, natural, tactile materials, comfortable furniture and good access to high-quality outdoor space all play a part in the creation of spaces that people choose to use.

The potential social, recreational and health benefits of shared outdoor spaces are significant. Physical and visual connections with the wider world matter too. Lessons can be learned from the traditional, three-sided almshouse where the semi-enclosed courtyard is often outward looking.

> People naturally congregate where they feel most comfortable.

3.6 Summary

While most mainstream housing developments seek to minimise internal communal space, in specialised housing for older people, shared space is rightly seen as an important way to encourage social interaction as well as a practical way to provide meals and activities.

However, quality and quantity have tended to be conflated. Large, sparsely populated sitting areas have become a common phenomenon in extra care and retirement housing – sparking unkind comparisons with hotel lobbies. People naturally congregate where they feel most comfortable, and that is often in smaller, less formal spaces with some kind of focus – an engaging view, a kitchen table or a fireplace.

Configuring a large development as a series of households, in which small groups of residents

4.0 The importance of home

Most young city dwellers now live in apartments; many others will have flat-shared as students or young professionals. Future generations of older people will be therefore accustomed to accessing their home via a communal entrance and a corridor, and managing with a balcony rather than a garden, before they grow old.

But it is important to remember that many of today's older people will have lived in a house for their entire life; perhaps not the same house, but a self-contained home on more than one floor, with a front door and a garden. The prospect of moving to an apartment, whether within a mainstream or specialised development, may create psychological barriers, despite the promise of removing physical ones. The challenge for designers is therefore to create practical, accessible, care-ready environments that look and feel like home, are adaptable to changing needs and will continue to delight.

↑ Stairs are a healthy option
and a straight flight will easily
accommodate a stair-lift. The
architects of Shawm House
have also made provision for a
through-floor lift (see p 88).

4.1 Making level choices

HOUSING TYPOLOGIES

For some young, working professionals, home is seen
as little more than a 'base'– somewhere to eat and sleep.
For older people, it will have come to mean much more
and that is partly what makes it so difficult to relinquish.

Houses remain very popular. Living on two or more
levels increases the privacy between rooms and 'going
upstairs to bed' is normal for many of us. We can exploit
volume and enjoy split levels in a house, but stairs are an
obvious physical barrier and a potential hazard. The most
serious accidents involving people over 65 usually occur
on the stairs or in the kitchen. Falls from stairs or steps
account for the largest proportion of accidents in the
home, and more than 60% of accidental home deaths
are associated with stairs.[63] Straight flights are safer than
those with winders and when designing for older people
it is also advisable to allow for a through-floor home-lift
(as well as a stair-lift) and not exceed two storeys.

For 'older olds' and those seeking a permanent
move it makes a great deal of sense to live on one level.
For many, the image that conjures up is a bungalow.
Combining many of the best attributes of a house and
apartment, bungalows have the unique advantage
of allowing volume (and top-lighting) to be exploited
throughout the home. They remain a good solution
where the scale is appropriate, and the budget allows,
either as a mainstream housing option or within a
retirement village.

→ Top-lighting and
high ceilings make all the
difference to the open
plan living spaces of new
bungalows in Greenwich
(Case Study 3).

→ Example of an efficient courtyard bungalow capable of matching densities achieved by two/three storey suburban housing.

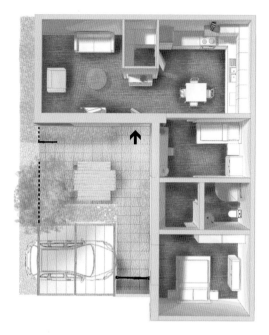

But traditional bungalow models are land-hungry and maintenance-heavy. Contemporary alternatives, including back-to-back, courtyard designs are capable of achieving respectable densities. Articulated footprints work particularly well. An L shape creates a small terrace with potential access from at least two rooms. This sheltered space can be at the back, where it will be more private, or at the front, where it will be part of the streetscape. A T shape can provide both.

Lift-served apartments are a much more realistic option in urban and suburban settings and the only viable solution in city centres. Apartments are usually step-free, safer and more secure, easier to heat and clean, require less maintenance and often enjoy longer views. Even in mainstream developments, neighbours are guaranteed. They also have the potential to offer greater flexibility in terms of how the internal space is used. Bedrooms and living spaces are often interchangeable (see Case Study 13), and the use of non-loadbearing partitions facilitates different spatial arrangements.

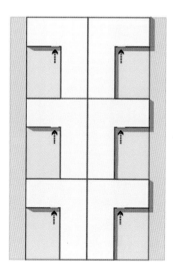

← A group of six bungalows illustrates the efficiency of this typology.

EXAMPLE | Flexible 1.5 bedroom apartment, Whiteley Village expansion

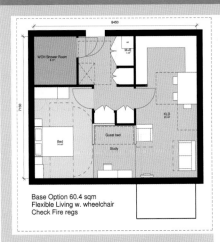

Base Option 60.4 sqm
Flexible Living w. wheelchair
Check Fire regs

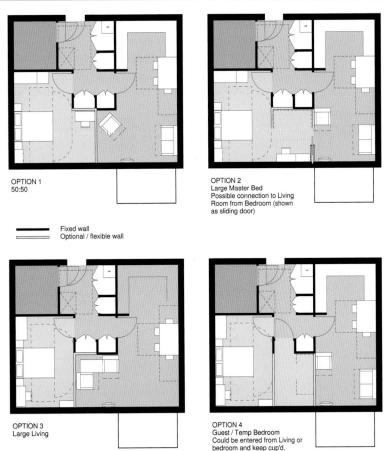

OPTION 1
50:50

OPTION 2
Large Master Bed
Possible connection to Living
Room from Bedroom (shown
as sliding door)

▬▬▬ Fixed wall
▭▭▭ Optional / flexible wall

OPTION 3
Large Living

OPTION 4
Guest / Temp Bedroom
Could be entered from Living or
bedroom and keep cup'd.

This simple apartment layout developed by Levitt Bernstein can be easily adapted for use in different ways; converting, for example, from an independent living arrangement to an en suite care environment. Different arrangements can be offered from the start, and homes can also be adapted later.

4.2 Practical and beautiful living spaces

DELIGHT IN THE FAMILIAR

Older people spend 70–90% of their time at home.[64] The proportion roughly equates to our age – 70% at 70, 80% at 80, and 90% at 90. In a mainstream home, most of that time will be spent in one room – our 'living room' – often alone. Even in developments with communal facilities, at least half of every day will tend to be spent in the private apartment.

Designers therefore have a responsibility to create living spaces that will not only be comfortable throughout the year, but will continue to delight. They must be practical and allow for personalisation. When we move, we generally want to take our furniture with us. Downsizing forces us to be selective. It can be even more important to take a favourite chair – or rug, or desk, or whatever else brings comfort and familiarity – with us.

Pelmets and mantelpieces used to be common features – opportunities to display treasured possessions, holiday souvenirs, and school photos

→ A personalised living space that looks and feels like home, (New Ground, Case Study 4).

of the grandchildren. While 'de-cluttering' may seem sensible to 'the family', and clean white spaces seductive to designers, we should not impose our values on others. Recent research by Demos looked at the pull and push factors that affect downsizing and found that concerns about the moving process itself and the need to cull possessions are significant barriers.[65]

The general trend towards more open plan living makes a great deal of sense for older people. Internal walls and doors are useful when different activities routinely need to take place in parallel or when it is impractical to heat an entire home, but they are much

← Space to display 'treasured possessions', (New Ground, Case Study 4).

← Flexible two-roomed apartment (Ørestad Retirement Home, Case Study 13).

less useful for single people, especially wheelchair users and others with restricted mobility. A conventional hall is also less important because the shared entrance lobby deals with muddy shoes and wheels.

Semi-open plan layouts (two linked spaces or a combined living, eating and cooking space that can be easily subdivided) provide useful flexibility. Where the escape route is not protected from the kitchen by a door, a sprinkler system will usually be required. Most specialised housing schemes will be fire-engineered and adopt a 'stay-put' strategy for means of escape but expert advice must always be sought (see p 58).

↑ The upside-down living space on the first floor of Shawm House enjoys spectacular views of Northumberland (see p 88).

4.3 Kitchens, bedrooms, bathrooms and storage

KITCHENS

Small kitchens were a drawback of much sheltered housing, and they are often still undersized. While we may cook less frequently as we age, we need more space to move around, open cupboards and use appliances. A mid-height, built-in oven (centre line 900–1000mm above floor level) with a pull-out shelf is safer and easier to use than a conventional low-level oven. It is important to provide worktops on both sides of the sink and hob, and at least one side of the oven and other tall items such as the fridge/freezer. Wall cupboards with drop-down shelving are useful too. A number of manufacturers produce kitchen ranges specifically for older and disabled people, and designers who specialise in this field go further, incorporating lighting within kitchen drawers for example.

↑ Practical and contemporary kitchen at Shawm House.

BEDROOMS

Self-contained bedrooms (with partitions and a door) are still generally considered preferable to a fully open-plan layout. This may change but a sliding partition between the main bedroom and the living space offers a flexible compromise, particularly for people who need to spend significant time in bed. The first of the HAPPI design principles (see p 18) calls for three habitable rooms, implying two bedrooms. Recent research confirms that many would-be downsizers consider this to be essential, though one bedroomed flats often still predominate.[66]

← Master bedroom in converted stable block, at Shawm House.

SPECIALIST | Accessible bathroom design

Accessible bathroom specialist, Motionspot, was established by friends Ed Warner and James Taylor after James was paralysed in a diving accident in 2005. After eight months in Stoke Mandeville Hospital, James returned home but was frustrated by the clinical looking, functional adaptations that had been installed to give him independence.

Driven by an ambition to provide a better alternative, the Motionspot ethos is to design and supply beautiful, accessible bathrooms that feel like a home environment and can adapt to suit the changing needs of individuals as they age. Design features include step-free shower floors, stylish slip-resistant floor tiles, integrated hand grips in basins, removable grab rails and shower seats, bi-folding glass shower enclosures and intuitive showers and basin mixers.

Ed Warner believes that digital technology will play an important role in the future of accessible bathrooms in the home:

Advanced 'wash & dry toilets' are becoming increasingly popular, and along with digital shower controls, lighting and heating that can all be operated from a phone or tablet, digital technology holds the key for delivering improved access for all at home.[67]

BATHROOMS

A well-designed bathroom is often the key to maintaining dignity and independence. Until very recently, hospital-style bathrooms have made bathing a procedure rather than a pleasure for older and disabled people, but safety and practicality no longer need to come at the expense of style.

Wet-rooms with a dedicated shower area, drained to a floor gulley, are now routinely expected. The showering space should be at least 1200mm square, located in a corner away from the door, and with access from two sides. A fold-down seat is typically provided on one wall with controls on the other. Full- or half-height screens, or a weighted curtain, are often fitted to increase privacy and reduce splashing. To provide the flexibility to accommodate individual preferences, the room should be large enough to allow a bath to be fitted over the shower space.

The shower room should be close to the main bedroom but opinion varies as to whether it should be en suite or accessed from circulation space. While access from both is often advocated, two doors can compromise the space or the layout of smaller shower rooms. As stumbling in the dark is the main risk, bed-head lighting controls that allow lights to be switched on before getting up make en suite provision less necessary.

STORAGE

Copious built-in storage allows living spaces and bedrooms to be more accessible, more attractive and less cluttered, reducing tripping and falls. Older people need more storage than younger people, not less, and the physical configuration is important. Numerous smaller, shallower cupboards are more practical than a single, deep one, and space within easy reach (700–1350mm above floor level) is safer and more useful.

Age-friendly homes should allow for at least one wheelchair to be stored inside the home. Mobility scooters are more difficult; while many people would like to store their scooter very close to the entrance to their home, this is generally only practical where home is a house or a bungalow and a secure, well-lit, covered space is feasible. In specialised housing, it is sensible to provide a fire-protected, communal scooter store close to the main entrance, ideally directly connected to the draught lobby where one is provided. The room should allow for wheelchair storage too, as many people will need to transfer from chair to scooter. Additional, lift-served basement storage should be considered for bulky items of furniture.

4.4 Stable and controllable internal conditions

DEALING WITH EXTREMES IN TEMPERATURE

Chapter 1.0 looked at how our body changes as we age (see p 6). In extreme weather, our reduced ability to regulate our body temperature makes us vulnerable to anything from mild discomfort to a life-threatening condition. Creating a thermally stable and controllable internal environment is therefore extremely important. While winter cold and fuel poverty remain very real concerns in older homes, overheating is now the greater threat in most new homes.

↓ Moveable external shutters on the balconies at St Bede's, help to reduce overheating and provide privacy.

INSIGHT | Mitigating overheating

Climate change is anticipated to cause an increase in extreme weather events, including heatwaves. Epidemiological studies conducted in the UK and France show that mortality during heatwaves is highest among those living in residential and nursing homes, despite the presence of carers.[i] However, until very recently there has been little recognition of older people's vulnerability to heat in the design and management of purpose-built older people's housing; instead, the emphasis has been on protecting them from cold.

Concern about the adverse impacts of cold still informs the design of older people's housing through the selection of heating systems and associated controls,[ii] and the management practices, such as keeping the heating on throughout the year.[iii] Such practices could be contributing to excess heat during heatwaves. Interviews with older occupants and monitoring of housing schemes indicate that new-build housing can be too warm during summer months, even outside of exceptional events.

The uncomfortably hot conditions experienced reflect the general lack of priority given to heatwaves, and are related to financial and regulatory factors. In new buildings, high levels of thermal insulation are generally required by Building Regulations in order to limit heat loss and thereby reduce heating demand, in turn minimising carbon emissions.

Without adequate ventilation, highly insulated buildings can trap heat. With opening windows on two sides, dual aspect dwellings can provide effective through-ventilation but are often seen as financially unviable (more expensive and less efficient in terms of land use) than double-banked corridors with single aspect apartments each side. Sunlight also contributes to internal heat gains. In contrast to Continental Europe where external solar shading is commonplace, in many UK housing schemes the only form of solar shading is internal blinds and curtains, often fitted by the occupants.[iv]

Providing adequate ventilation to single-aspect rooms and apartments, while allowing restricted window opening for safety reasons, is a significant challenge, requiring a number of mitigating strategies. Recent research suggests that buildings with a high thermal mass (designed to allow the fabric to absorb heat during the heat of the day before being dissipated at night via ventilation) perform better than lighter weight solutions. Traditional brick and block construction with concrete floors and wet-plaster internal finishes, combined with windows with multiple opening lights to increase ventilation, is a sound starting point. Other measures include ensuring that internal heating and hot water pipes are well insulated (particularly in corridors) using a Building Management System to control corridor windows and doors, and providing internal stack vents to apartments to increase ventilation.

In addition, external solar shading (including awnings, movable shutters and trees) and reflective paving offer passive ways to reduce internal solar heat gain by tackling the growing problem of summer overheating at source.

Dr Alan Lewis, lecturer in architecture at the School of Environment, Education and Development, University of Manchester.

Notes

i Kovats, S.R., Johnson, H. and Griffiths, C. (2006) 'Mortality in Southern England during the 2003 heat wave by place of death', *Health Statistics Quarterly*, 29: 6–8; Fouillet, A., Rey, G., Laurent, F., Pavillon, G., Bellec, S., Guihenneuc-Jouyaux, C., Clavel, J., Jougla, E. and Hemon, D. (2006) 'Excess mortality related to the August 2003 heat wave in France', *International Archives of Occupational and Environmental Health*, 80: 16–24.
ii Lewis, A. (2015) 'Designing for an imagined user: Provision for thermal comfort in energy-efficient extra-care housing', *Energy Policy*. 84: 204–212.
iii, iv Gupta, R., Walker, G., Lewis, A., Barnfield, L., Gregg, M., Neven, L. (2016) *Care Provision Fit for a Future Climate*, York: Joseph Rowntree Foundation.

Behaviour remains an important component. Vulnerable residents may need help to select appropriate clothing and remove or add layers as the temperature fluctuates. Cold food and drinks should be available in summer and warm food and drinks in winter. The shoulder seasons (spring and autumn) can be the most difficult as the daily temperature variation can be considerable. A report produced for the Joseph Rowntree Foundation recommended that extra care developments and care homes should provide at least one lounge area in which the temperature can remain comfortable in extreme weather, even if that requires mechanical cooling.[68]

LOW CARBON, SUSTAINABLE APPROACHES

There has been a tendency to treat housing for older people as a special case, exempt from energy targets and other environmental targets. But this is changing, and rightly so. Climate change is one of the greatest challenges we face and there are many good reasons why this sector should lead the way in terms of sustainability – not least the fact that the homes and supporting spaces are intensively used, often by vulnerable people. Passive measures remain the best approach.

EXAMPLE | St Loyes, Exeter

The client for this planned extra care scheme, which is part of the Millbrook Care Village, was was committed to a sustainable solution that reduced overall energy use and provided free heating to residents. Focusing on a rigorous 'fabric-first' approach that optimises solar gain, Architype and its client adopted a Passivhaus design to meet these objectives and provide a healthy and comfortable environment. Using Exeter University's PROMETHEUS weather data up to 2080, the scheme adopts the council's *Design for Future Climate Change* requirements to improve its long-term resilience. It also takes account of Building Biology recommendations to reduce physical, chemical and biological risks and eliminate toxic materials and electro-magnetic radiation, to create a natural, healthy living environment through the specification of a palette of natural material finishes.

EXAMPLE | Shawm House, Northumberland

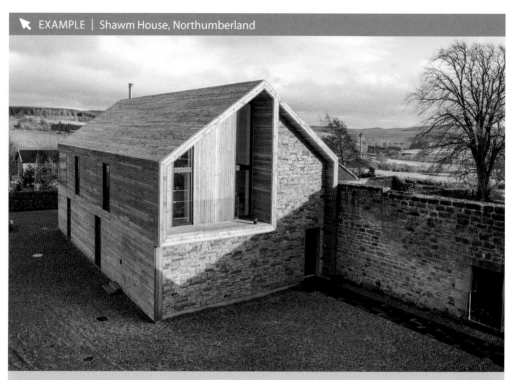

Passivhaus principles have also informed the design of Shawm House, a bespoke two-storey house designed by MawsonKerr Architects. The project was commissioned (and later built) by the client for his ageing parents. It utilises super-insulation to both the new and existing elements, triple glazing throughout, and a highly airtight construction that surpasses Passivhaus standards. This is coupled with the use of integrated, renewable technologies such as PVs and a biomass boiler to provide heating and hot water during the summer and winter respectively. These combined measures reduce heating costs to a minimum. Rainwater harvesting, attention to accessible design and design for low maintenance inside and out all contribute to the holistic and sustainable environment enjoyed by the ageing owners.

4.5 Private outdoor space for year-round enjoyment

GARDENS AND PATIOS

Private outdoor space is immensely enjoyable, provided that it is manageable. For individual houses and bungalows this need only be a small garden or patio with small areas of planting (preferably raised), space for a table and chairs, somewhere to store a few tools and a mix of sun and shade (see p 45 and p 78). Hard paving is better than timber decking, and gravel should always be avoided.

Ground floor apartments also benefit from a small, private patio. These will often adjoin a communal garden, and a section of low wall or raised planter allowing views and access to the shared space beyond is more sociable and attractive than a continuous fence, and worth the compromise in terms of privacy.

BALCONIES AND ROOF TERRACES

Communal amenity space does not obviate the need for private outdoor space, but a sizeable balcony connected to the living space is often enough. In most situations a fully or partially inset balcony, or a winter garden, will be more appropriate than an exposed cantilevered balcony. In certain cases, such as specialised dementia facilities, private balconies may be considered unsafe.

↑ Semi-enclosed private patio at Pilgrim Gardens.

While north-facing balconies should generally be avoided as they receive no sun, south or west-facing spaces need to provide some shade. A retractable awning or sliding screen should be considered for projecting balconies. The sliding panels in the winter gardens at Lime Tree Court (see p 38 and Case Study 7) possibly represent the ultimate solution, but are expensive. The design of the balustrading, and the handrail, must maintain safety while maximising views out when seated. The design and detailing are important, as the eye level of a seated wheelchair user is typically 900–1300mm above floor level, and a balustrade, 1100mm.

Circadian House, a modest but charming single-storey home in Cambridge, designed by now retired professor of architecture Dean Hawkes, for himself and his wife in the 1990s, embodies many of the simple qualities discussed in this chapter. As Professor Hawkes explains in the Viewpoint opposite, its orientation and its relationship with the garden contribute to a series of spaces that continue to bring delight and support the natural circadian rhythm.

← Private semi-outdoor space at Windmill Court, Chingford, London. (PRP for Circle Housing Group, now part of Clarion Housing Group).

💬 VIEWPOINT | Living in harmony with the seasons

On 23 December 1991 my wife and I moved into a small house that I had designed for a site in the suburbs of Cambridge. We were then in our 50s and, over the last 25 years we, and the house, have aged together. This summary outlines the principles that informed the design and offers a brief and personal 'post-occupancy evaluation' of the house as it has sustained and delighted us.

The key to the plan is its orientation. The site at the end of a suburban cul-de-sac is a narrow rectangle with its long axis almost east–west. The approach is from the west through a courtyard behind a sheltering screen wall. Almost all of the accommodation is in a long, low block on the northern boundary. The entrance is between this and a flat-roofed block to the south.

The main block contains two bedrooms, the kitchen, bathrooms and a closet, with a study in the flat-roofed block. A second, much smaller study stands at the east end of the small courtyard garden. With the exception of the guest bedroom, the entire house enjoys a direct connection to the garden. A timber and glass screen extends across the face of living room and principal bedroom. In the living room this incorporates a tall bay window.

The effect of this is that life in the house is informed and inspired by a sense of the passage of time, diurnally and seasonally, as the sun follows its course from east to west. This experience is reinforced by the intimate connection between the principal rooms and the garden that is enjoyed visually at all seasons and becomes an extension of the interior in the summer months.

Each morning we wake in our book-lined bedroom at the east end of the house, nearest to the morning light, and move to eat breakfast at a small table in the bay window of the living room. The brightness and warmth of this place brings us alive ready for the day. At weekends, breakfast can be leisurely, but on weekdays we soon begin our daily rounds, sometimes at home, often away. What is important is that we each have our own space – the two studies, where we spend much time.

At lunch we are back to the table in the bay window, on bright days enjoying the warmth of the sun. In high summer an alternative is to eat at a small table in the garden, in the shade of the tall hawthorns on the south boundary. Afternoons follow the same pattern as mornings; either out of the house or at work in our studies.

The most enjoyable aspect of our lives in the house is the sense of nature, of the passage of time that it captures by the observance of simple principles of orientation. This is also at the heart of the idea of the 'Circadian House'. When the house was built we were in vigorous middle age; now, a quarter of a century later, our way of life has inevitably changed. We've retired and grown older, although thankfully we remain physically active. Nonetheless we live in what I call a changed 'environmental envelope'. We are less tolerant of high and low temperatures. We need brighter light for visual tasks such as reading and writing. Our hearing is less acute than before. This little house continues to sustain us. Most important it brings delight to our lives.

Dean Hawkes, architect and Emeritus Professor of Architectural Design at Cardiff University and Emeritus Fellow of Darwin College, Cambridge.

4.6 Accessibility and internal space standards

ACCESSIBILITY

Though widely used by the World Health Organization, the term 'age-friendly housing' is not recognised by either the planning system or Building Regulations in England, and is therefore not subject to specific standards. However, Lifetime Homes, now owned by Habinteg Housing Association, was conceived, and has been recognised, as an age-friendly standard.[69] Habinteg has also been responsible for the widely used *Wheelchair Housing Design Guide*, now on its third edition.[70]

As we saw in Chapter 1.0, for planning and building control purposes these standards have been effectively replaced by new 'optional requirements' defined in the Building Regulations but invoked through planning. Category 2 (or M4(2) Accessible and adaptable housing – similar to Lifetime Homes) is the minimum standard that should be considered for any housing designed for older people – many argue, the minimum standard for all new homes.

For specialised housing, some clients require a large proportion of dwellings to meet Category 2, and the remainder to meet Category 3 (or M4(3) Wheelchair user housing); some require all Category 3; others again (perhaps the majority) consider somewhere between Category 2 and Category 3 to be appropriate across the board. To complicate things further, many clients add their own functional requirements.

↓ Three versions of the same generic 2 bedroom 4 person apartment layout showing the required features and spatial implications.

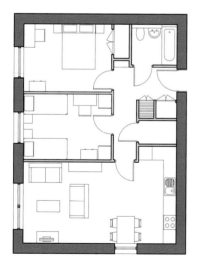

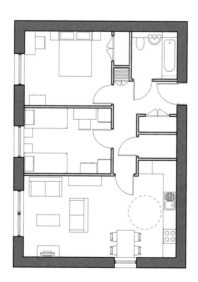

Category 1, 2 and 3 (left to right)

Table of Space Standards				
	1p	**1b2p**	**2b3p**	**2b4p**
NDSS (m²)	37/39	50	61	70
Extra Care (m²)	not appropriate	55–58	67–72	76–82

SPACE STANDARDS

Here too, generic guidance is difficult but it is widely accepted that the minimum gross (internal) floor areas (GIAs) set out in the Nationally Described Space Standard (NDSS) should be exceeded by at least 10% for age-friendly one and two bedroom apartments.[71]

As a general rule, the main bedroom should be at least 12.5m² (NDSS requires 11.5m²) and storage at least 2m² in one bedroom apartments and at least 2.5m² in two beds (NDSS requires 1.5m² and 2m² respectively).

4.7 Summary

'Home' is an emotive subject. As we age, the practical advantages of living on one level with relatively few doors and flexible spaces that flow are irrefutable. Rising density and land cost demand that we live on top of each other, and common sense tells us that we should offload the burden of maintenance. But our head often says one thing, and our heart another. Designers have to demonstrate that well-designed apartments with protected balconies,

winter gardens or roof terraces, are not only the most sensible homes for the majority of older people, they can also be the most desirable.

A combination of the NDSS and the optional accessibility requirements in Part M provides a reasonable starting point for mainstream age-friendly housing. While most 'younger olds' could manage reasonably well in a well-designed Category 2 home, 'older olds' would do well to seek the extra space and accessibility of Category 3. In specialised housing, the baseline should be set somewhere between the two, and space standards increased accordingly.

While the 'rules' in these documents will achieve sensible bathrooms, wide enough doors and handles and controls that are within reach, regulation tends not to be forward-looking, and there are no rules for beauty, delight, flexibility or choice. It is easy to lose sight of the importance of home, particularly when designing a large, complex building, but vital to step back, look at each dwelling in turn and imagine how it would feel to spend up to 90% of every day in those one or two spaces, throughout the year.

5.0 Responding to a changing world

This chapter looks at the importance of consolidating what can be learned from the past while contemplating the future. It highlights the importance of research, working with end users and learning from built projects, while considering how our lives are continually changing as a result of demographic change, global pressures and the digital revolution.

Technology has already changed the way we communicate and is becoming much more prevalent within the home. Product design has become extremely sophisticated and even everyday household items are becoming smarter and more multifunctional. While some of this may seem peripheral to the subject of age-friendly housing, much of it will impact on how we live, how our homes are designed, and how our health is monitored and our care delivered.

5.1 Designing for future need and expectation

CHANGING LIFESTYLES

Although some demographic shifts have been predictable, others have taken even the experts by surprise. Gender equality has rapidly increased, more women are working; more men are participating in childcare and domestic chores; across the board, stereotypes are gradually being eroded. Marriage rates are dropping and divorce rates rising; we have more fluid relationships, accepting perhaps that it may be unrealistic to expect a monogamous relationship to last for 80 years. We generally expect more choice and more control over our lives.

Across the western world, we are having fewer children too, but despite this, and the fact that we have more labour-saving gadgets, we seem to have less time. We are arguably more sociable but we socialise differently – more with friends than with neighbours, more spontaneously and less routinely. Our plans are often more fluid – we can text to say we are running late and order a takeaway or taxi from our smartphone at a moment's notice. We have larger social networks; we keep in touch through social media and we share much more information about our lives. We can talk to hundreds, maybe thousands, of people we don't even know at the same time, and we can find out what is going on anywhere in the world at the click of a button.

INNOVATION IN DESIGN FOR DEMENTIA

Chapter 4.0 mentioned that simple acts, such as hanging out the washing or feeding chickens, often evoke positive memories for older people with dementia. Future generations will have different memories; unloading the tumble drier and 'feeding' the Tamagotchi may feel less therapeutic but could prove equally evocative.[73]

In 2011, Design Council CABE and the Department of Health launched *Living Well with Dementia*, a design competition seeking ideas to improve the lives of those affected by the disease.[74] The aim was to design and develop products and services that rethink living with dementia, and launch them as real initiatives:

We wanted to find better ways for those affected by dementia to live well in their homes and to improve their overall quality of life. We also wanted to reduce the need for expensive hospital care and alleviate the feelings of isolation and fear that often accompany diagnosis.

ℹ INFO | Newcastle City Futures

The Newcastle City Futures project was established in 2014 by Newcastle University as a collaborative platform to bring together research and development potential with long-term policy trends and business needs in the city. Its Future Homes Project is developing forward-looking housing exemplars that will combine in one place innovations in flexible living, materials, digital technology and zero-/low-energy systems to provide supportive homes for everyone at any life-stage.[72]

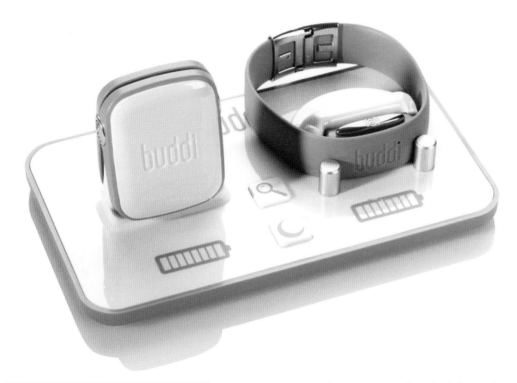

← Buddi wristband
alarm set.

*Our brief pointed out three areas of opportunity
regarding people with dementia and their carers:*

1. How might we make their lives easier?
*2. How might we help them prepare so as to
maintain quality of life and deal with crises?*
*3. How might we enable them to make the
most of life?*

Five winners were chosen from over 2,000 entries:

- **Grouple** – a secure, private online social hub
  helping people share the responsibilities of caring
  for a loved one.
- **Ode** – a fragrance-release system designed to
  stimulate appetite among people with dementia.
- **Dementia Dog** – assistance dogs that help people
  with dementia lead more fulfilled, independent
  and stress-free lives.
- **Trading Times** – an online service that matches
  carers and older adults with local businesses for
  flexible paid work.
- **Buddi** – a wristband personal alarm that can send
  alerts from anywhere to Buddi's support services.

All focus on and around the point of diagnosis, aiming
to be preventative measures that improve the quality
of life in the early stages of dementia for the increasing
numbers of people diagnosed. They demonstrate the
vast potential of innovative ideas in an underserved
market and show how design can play a key role in
confronting a major social challenge.

5.2 Appropriate use of technology

REMAINING IN CONTROL

As we saw in Chapter 3.0, technology is likely to play an increasingly important role in providing health and care support, and in connecting people. This may include the mainstreaming of technology-enabled care services such as home health-monitoring tools, digital voice-activated devices to enable people to control their home environment, the increasing and more sophisticated use of health data to improve clinical treatments, and the use of social media to create and sustain online communities with shared interests.

INCREASING CONNECTIVITY

Connectivity will be increasingly important to the health and wellbeing of an ageing population. It should be considered in a holistic way that includes physical mobility, transport, the built environment, the virtual world and the physical–virtual intersection.

One of the most striking impacts of the digital revolution has been its ability to facilitate social connectivity. This has been most evident among younger people but it has the potential to alleviate some of the loneliness that many older people experience. A total of 70% of people aged between 65 and 74 are online; using email and video calling services such as Skype to remain in contact

 INSIGHT | The potential for technology to support an ageing population

The rapid evolution of medical and assistive technologies makes predicting the scale of their impact difficult. The speed of development creates a need for new methods of evaluation of these technologies. While technologies that assist in health and care could significantly increase short-term costs, they potentially reduce costs significantly in the medium and long term. The savings will depend on the type of technology, for example whether they treat symptoms, prevent disease, change behaviour, radically innovate or incrementally improve, and how they are implemented. The extent to which the savings can be understood, and therefore justified, depends largely on how the benefits are measured.

Developments such as 3D-printed joints and organs, therapeutic robotics and genomics have enormous potential to improve health outcomes across the population, while improvements in personalised ('precision') and stratified medicine may allow better

targeting of medicines, making treatments more cost-effective. Increases in real-time data collection, driven by developments in wearable technology and other forms of telemonitoring will enable healthcare professionals to provide more appropriate treatment and support for patients and carers, while the resulting large datasets could drive forward research in many areas and potentially improve prevention and early intervention.

Technology, such as alarms, home monitoring systems and GPS locators can help carers locate people with dementia. There is evidence that they are already using 'off the shelf' technologies, such as baby monitors and smartphone-based GPS tracking apps, in supporting people living with dementia. Specialised technology could be used more widely and more effectively, but this inevitably raises ethical issues.

Text adapted from Future of an Ageing Population, *published by the Government Office for Science.*[75]

with their family members and friends. Evidence suggests that this impacts positively on their level of participation in voluntary social, religious and political activities, clubs and organisations.[76]

More sophisticated technologies, such as augmented reality services, can facilitate virtual participation in a wide range of activities such as social events, the pursuit of hobbies or virtual tourism. Older people, especially those who are geographically isolated or have limited mobility, could benefit by feeling more connected, empowered and independent through the use of digital technology to access information, services and social networks.

There is broad agreement that wearable technology and systems that can be operated by Wi-Fi and smartphone technology have the most potential and this requires little permanent infrastructure within our homes. The compatibility and reliability of the systems and devices are paramount considerations, particularly where safety is involved.

THE NEED FOR ETHICAL DEBATE

These advances are not without risk. Digital technology is often used to reinforce existing social contacts, rather than build new ones, and could inadvertently lead to a breakdown in traditional forms of social interaction. There is also increasing concern about the targeting and exploitation of older and more vulnerable people as a result of internet fraud and computer hacking.

Experts agree that we must remain in control of technology rather than allow it to control us. As a society we must exercise choice about what we develop; as individuals we must remain free to choose how we use technology ourselves and how

it is used on our behalf. Used well, it will increase the control we have over our lives by supporting privacy and independence as well as increasing our social networks. But it can also be pervasive, even controlling; leading to a different kind of dependency. Where and how data is stored, who should have access to it and who best represents the interests of people who are unable to make rational decisions or express their own wishes, are issues that must form part of a wider, ethical discussion.

The debate around assisted suicide is also relevant, as is the question of whether it is necessarily right to offer expensive, risky or invasive treatments to prolong the lives of people who are very old or very ill.

> **Experts agree that we must remain in control of technology rather than allow it to control us.**

⬇ Grandmother and grand-daughter communicating on FaceTime by tablet.

5.3 Learning from experience

DESIGNING WITH END USERS

Designers are sometimes accused of arrogance – believing they know best rather than listening to the end user. Paradoxically, though most people feel more strongly about their own home than about any other building they will ever use, very few housing architects ever manage to meet the end users of new housing. Only cohousing (see Case Studies 4 and 5) and bespoke design (see Shawm House, p 88) offer these very personal opportunities.

When new housing is planned in established communities, such as estate regeneration projects, it is usually possible to talk to at least some of the residents who will remain or return. Though neither the designers nor the residents know exactly who will live where, through discussion, workshops and other forms of co-design, valuable insight and ideas can be gained.

From the start, Lodge Road (Case Study 12) offered some opportunity for co-design because its purpose was to rehouse residents decanted from Dora House, the tired 1960s sheltered housing block occupying the site. The small bedsits, which were failing to meet the needs of its residents, will be replaced with a wide range of new accommodation; designed to give residents the security of a 'home for life'. A similar opportunity arose in Bermondsey Spa (opposite).

➜ Front cover of DWELL research project publication *Designing with downsizers*.

THE CONTRIBUTION OF RESEARCH

We can also learn a great deal through published research. Recent, wide-ranging work coordinated by the ARCC (Adaptation and Resilience in the Context of Change network) hosted by the Environmental Change Institute, University of Oxford, focused on health and wellbeing.[77]

It includes the University of Sheffield's DWELL research project (Designing for Wellbeing in Environments for Later Life, see pp 100, 102–5). This was carried out over a three-year period alongside Sheffield residents, communities, and professional stakeholders.[78] The downsizing strand of the research had two main aims: to explore third-agers' housing aspirations; and to use this knowledge to generate a series of speculative design proposals using a participatory co-design process. The methodology and the outcomes are published in *Designing with Downsizers*.[79]

EXAMPLE | Bermondsey Spa, London

In 2006, prompted by the extension of the Jubilee Line, plans to provide 350 new homes in a run-down part of Bermondsey necessitated the demolition of a sheltered housing scheme. Ten of its residents needed to be rehoused in the first phase of the new development but because the plans included new shops and a new health centre, and public transport had substantially improved, the residents were happy in principle to move into mainstream accommodation.

The developer, Hyde Housing, and architects, Levitt Bernstein, worked directly with the group to establish their hopes and needs. Their modest requests – to remain together, retain a view of the beautiful, Grade II* listed, St James's Church, have their own entrance and lift and stair core – were accommodated in the design. The scheme was one of the first in London to provide 100% Lifetime Homes. The ten flats for the older residents go slightly further in terms of accessibility (mainly in relation to bathroom provision) but are indistinguishable externally.

INSIGHT | Designing with Downsizers: key findings and research methodology

Research questions and methods

The research process began with a series of open questions for participants and stakeholders:

- What type(s) of housing would attract you to downsize?

- Why do you think the market has been slow to react to demand from downsizers?

- How can a home support or enhance your current and future lifestyle, or adapt to unexpected changes in health and mobility?

- How can a home adapt to diverse and multigenerational household types?

- How can a home contribute to the creation of vibrant, sustainable, and mixed-age urban neighbourhoods?

- What is the role and contribution of design in this process?

These questions were addressed through a mixed-methods approach to draw out different forms of knowledge and practice:

- A review of existing housing design guidance and standards.

- Home visits, interviews and focus groups with around 150 Sheffield residents to better understand the everyday experience of third and fourth-agers.

- Interviews with 20 housing professionals and developers from the social and private sector.

Co-design

The design elements of the DWELL research were carried out alongside a core group of participants who either had personal experience of downsizing, or a future aspiration to downsize. The group included people in their 50s, 60s, 70s and 80s, from a range of different tenures and backgrounds. Participants were involved in a regular series of focus group discussions, design workshops and study visits over a period of six months to develop a brief for downsizer homes, followed by hands-on involvement in the design and review of downsizer typologies. The aim of this process was to go further than a guidance or 'checklist' approach, and to demonstrate the value of design as a research tool to both produce and represent new knowledge.

Findings

The available evidence suggests that many households would be keen to downsize in later life if there were attractive options available in the right locations. The research also found strong demand amongst third-agers for better quality and more accessible homes located in 'normal' streets and neighbourhoods, where they can continue to participate in mixed-age communities.

While it is apparent that there is no one 'ideal' downsizer home, a number of common themes emerged from this co-design process:

- Demand for accessible single storey or two storey typologies, with a continuing appetite for bungalow typologies (despite their apparent unpopularity with planners and developers).

- A willingness to consider apartment living, as long as the offer feels secure, spacious and is in a good location, and potentially provides extra facilities such as allotments and shared space to host social events.

- Demand for fewer (bed) rooms but more space and adaptability to accommodate separate living, visiting friends and family, and grandchildren.

- Provision of manageable outdoor space for gardening and relaxation, such as courtyard gardens, roof terraces or generous balconies.

- The need for dedicated resident and visitor car parking provision in all but the most centrally located sites.

- Above all, a home that continues to allow people to pursue the pleasures of life today, while feeling secure that their home can adapt to their future needs.

Note

In the context of this report, 'downsizer homes' are defined as 'general needs housing (ie not age-exclusive or specialist retirement accommodation) that is more suited to the requirements and aspirations of third-agers.

> ... strong demand amongst third-agers for better quality and more accessible homes located in 'normal' streets and neighbourhoods.

> Design encompasses processes, systems, spaces, relationships and products. It is the overarching 'glue' that links many of our experiences together.

> We know what to do, so why aren't we doing it?

What does it mean to live well in older age? And what contribution can the built environment make in answering that question?

The DWELL project[i] spent three years researching these issues, with focus on the city of Sheffield. Involving researchers from architecture, planning, sociology and public health, we considered the complex set of interrelated forces that conjoin to create the environment around us, and how design interventions could have an impact on adjusting these to create better outcomes, not only for older people, but for society at large.

Design encompasses processes, systems, spaces, relationships and products. It is the overarching 'glue' that links many of our experiences together. But it is poorly understood, not least by our leaders, who regard it as the expensive ornamentation of technical solutions. Design, however, works across categories, connecting disparate types of information. It also works across scales, linking such aspects as transport, streetscape, neighbourhood planning and the design of homes – including digital communication and the internet of things – to make life work better for everyone. It can assist mobility and connectivity, as well as functionality and pleasure. These things may be difficult to measure financially, yet when they don't work well, they can have serious, long-lasting and expensive consequences.

There is a mass of knowledge about how to design for the older age group that includes regulations, guidance, recommendations, toolkits and manuals. Good designers and good built examples exist, as testified by the case studies in this report. Building on these and the reports of the HAPPI panel, the DWELL project produced a range of research including designs for housing and neighbourhoods, planning policy, data analysis informing Sheffield City Council's strategic goals, public realm improvements and co-design strategies involving older people themselves. Taken collectively, these outline the issues, provide the justification and showcase the solutions. We know what to do, so why aren't we doing it?

Our research found that the available solutions are restricted by the complexity of the built environment and the processes leading to development. If any of these fails, or don't join up, then the system breaks down. Developers specialising in older people's housing operate in a niche market, and government interventions are focused on the demand side, targeting first-time buyers. But DWELL's findings show that well-designed, user-focused housing for older people is actually suited to all people. Moreover, if offered suitable, good quality housing in the right place at the right price, many older people told us they would be eager to downsize. This would release family homes back into the market too.

We found that many older people aspire to dwellings and outdoor spaces that will safeguard residents' independence, being easy to maintain, with reasonable management charges and which offer easy connections to family, friends, cultural and social activities as a natural part of urban, suburban or rural life. Our research focused on how the environment could promote wellbeing and mobility, both concepts that embody self-respect and autonomy while enabling connections, mentally or physically, with the outside world. This includes an investment in the past, present and future, in nature's cycles, current affairs, the transcendent and the natural and built environment.

To achieve this is relatively simple in design terms, but to work best for older people it would lead to building slightly larger homes with attention paid to accessibility (level thresholds, lifts, mobility vehicle charging points etc.) while siting buildings in appropriate locations that offer good public transport options and cycling facilities. The scarcity of land leads to high costs in attractive locations, resulting in higher-density proposals that can lead to kick-back from local residents, while in low value areas only the Local Authority or its partners can attract the subsidies that will unlock development. In both cases this can work against diverse, integrated communities. We need new ways of subsidising housing that will make it worthwhile building genuinely for the life course, as this will help build inclusive, resilient neighbourhoods.

In our co-design work, our older participants were a diverse mix of people with many life skills, interests and opinions, with energy and enthusiasm, keen to participate in shaping the future city. In this respect, older people themselves can form part of the solution. This untapped resource could change the prevailing view of the ageing as needy and dependent. Making their voices heard through civic governance, action groups and consumer power, older people have the ability to set the agenda, influence the course of development and shape the way our cities might work successfully in the future. For, as our research found, if the design of housing and neighbourhoods were fit for the ageing, it would set a new standard that is good for everyone.

Note

i   DWELL stands for Designing for Wellbeing in Environments for Later Life. It was funded under the call Design for Wellbeing: Ageing and Mobility in the Built Environment by EPSRC, ESRC and AHRC. For further information visit www.dwell.group.shef.ac.uk

Sarah Wigglesworth RDI MBE, is a Director of Sarah Wigglesworth Architects and former Professor of Architecture at Sheffield University.

In *For Future Living: Innovative approaches to joining up housing and health*, IPPR North considered what people want from their housing as they age. What seems most surprising is that these simple priorities are not being met as a matter of course:

The key demands of older people are much the same as those of other people in the housing market: reasonable-sized houses, in good places, with modern fittings that are cheap to run.

What is also clear is that when health needs change, people appear to prefer to remain in their own home with support either in the home or in the community, rather than be transferred into institutional care facilities. This is not to imply that as people age they are not aware that where they presently live may not be appropriate forever or may need to be adapted. While they may be reluctant to plan their housing needs far in advance (Pannell et al 2012), our focus groups showed that people in the younger group (50–55) were aware of the potential changes to family size, income and health that might affect what they need from their accommodation and what compromises might be necessary.

The challenge for the market, social housing developers and policymakers is to develop housing both that people want to live in, and that permits people to live healthy, independent lives in their home for as long as possible… our current stock of housing falls well short of supporting either aim. [80]

> ...if offered suitable, good quality housing in the right place at the right price, many older people told us they would be eager to downsize.

> As our research found, if the design of housing and neighbourhoods were fit for the ageing, it would set a new standard that is good for everyone.

SATISFACTION SURVEYS

Satisfaction surveys of new homes are usually conducted soon after people have moved in. Comments are rarely differentiated by age but many of the issues raised are likely to be of particular concern to older people – further evidence that their needs are not being factored in to most new-build housing. Lack of daylight, small rooms and inadequate storage still tend to be among the most commonly cited shortcomings.

We know that sight loss is a natural symptom of ageing. People over 40 need twice as much light as 16 year olds to enjoy the same visual acuity.[81] NHS statistics show that 64% of registered blind and 66% of partially sighted people were aged 75 or over in 2011.[82] A review by Margaret Martin in 2013 found that the risk of falling downstairs is doubled for people with sight loss.[83]

POST OCCUPANCY EVALUATION (POE)

The aim of POE is to learn from experience and avoid repeating mistakes. There are two main strands: one involves monitoring building performance, and the other, gathering feedback from end users.

What Clients think of Architects, the results of survey conducted by Hawkins Brown for RIBA in 2016, revealed that designers scored very well on design, but less well in two other respects.[84] One concern was project management, and the other, the 'feedback loop'. The survey showed that clients are disappointed when architects 'walk away' at the end of a project, and value those who follow up when not contracted to do so. Clients also talked about the strength of evidence-based design and the desire to see work supported by proof from previous experience. This adds to growing calls for POE to become a mandatory element of the basic architectural service.

→ Older people are now central to debates about how to live well in later life.

The publication *Building Knowledge: Pathways to POE*, explains how POE:

- Delivers important benefits to both practice and clients
- Saves money
- Reduces waste and environmental impact
- Improves wellbeing
- Develops knowledge
- Can prove the value of good design.[85]

There is no formal protocol for conducting POE but toolkits developed to help evaluate design proposals may be helpful.

In specialised housing, staff and carers receive valuable anecdotal feedback from residents and visitors all the time. Some providers gather feedback on a structured basis, as do some organisations. The EAC (Elderly Accommodation Counsel) is particularly good at this, and the winning schemes in their annual awards are selected by residents, not housing or design professionals.[86]

---

i INFO | The EVOLVE toolkit

Produced by the universities of Sheffield and Kent, the EVOLVE tool *(Evaluation of Older People's Living Environments)* was designed to assess how well a building contributes to both the physical support of older people and their personal well-being. Developed from research in extra care housing, including schemes funded through the then Department of Health's Extra Care Housing Fund, it can also be applied to other types of development, including sheltered or mainstream housing. It consists of a set of checklists ordered in the sequence of the rooms or spaces encountered when walking through a building.[87]

---

i INFO | The King's Fund Enhanced Healing Environment (EHE) assessment toolkits

In order to help as many health and care organisations as possible to develop more supportive design for people with dementia, The King's Fund developed a suite of dementia-friendly assessment tools for use in four different care settings:

- Is your care home dementia friendly?
- Is your health centre dementia friendly?
- Is your housing dementia friendly?
- Is your ward dementia friendly? Is your hospital dementia friendly?

The work that informed the initial development of the resources, the EHE dementia care programme, was funded by the Department of Health to support the implementation of the National Dementia Strategy. Following the completion of the EHE programme, the work on dementia-friendly design is being taken forward by the Association for Dementia Studies (ADS), University of Worcester.[88]

5.4 New ways of thinking

THE COMMERCIAL OPPORTUNITIES OF UNIVERSAL DESIGN

In 2014, ILC-UK, in conjunction with the Engineering Design Centre at Cambridge University and the Institute of Engineering and Technology, sought to explore how design and technology could better respond to the challenges of ageing. Their report, *Opportunity Knocks: Designing solutions for an ageing society*, opens with a quote:

We are continually faced by great opportunities brilliantly disguised as insoluble problems.

John W. Gardner (1912–2002), American activist, author, and Secretary of Health, Education, and Welfare under President Lyndon Johnson (1912–2002).[89]

The report noted that:

… the technological revolution experienced over the past 20 years has happened alongside recognition of the opportunities and challenges of our ageing society…

… harnessing the power of good design and promoting innovative applications of technology will be essential in helping us meet the challenges of an ageing society…

The investigation began by looking at examples of products designed with older people in mind that had proved highly successful because of their universal appeal. In May 2015, the ILC-UK research team hosted an expert workshop to discuss the possibilities for technology and design in an ageing society. Participants were drawn from a diverse range of backgrounds; some were designers themselves or worked in the wider technology sphere, while others were specialists in the experiences of older people.

ℹ INFO | The Ford Approach

The original Ford Focus car was designed with the needs of older drivers specifically in mind. Designers were encouraged to wear the 'Third Age Suit'– a suit that simulated the effects of ageing. It stiffened joints, added bulk around the torso and added visual impairments such as cataracts.

The Focus has wider front doors and a higher seating position, which makes it easier to get in and out compared with the Ford Escort. It has more headroom, the controls are easier to reach and grasp, and the displays are more legible. The car went on to become the world's bestselling car, as well as winning 'Car of the Year' awards in both Europe and North America.[91]

Sam Farber founded OXO International in 1989 after watching his wife, who had arthritis in her hands, struggle to use many kitchen utensils. OXO commissioned a new range of kitchen utensils whose design was based on the principles of inclusive design. The design brief explicitly stated that the aim was to develop products with the broadest possible appeal, not just for consumers with specific needs.

The brand 'Good Grips' was born from this process. These products feature a handle design that does not rotate in the hand, is large enough to not strain the hand and also distributes the pressure across the hand when in use. The soft rubber fins designed for enhanced finger-grip also serve the dual purpose of making it clear to consumers that these products have been designed for ease of use. Even the design of the large, tapered hole for hanging the utensils was intended to make it easier for someone with poor vision or reduced coordination to use.

The first 20 Good Grips products were launched in 1990 and nearly 100 products have been added to the range since. Good design has propelled OXO to success, and from an initial turnover of £2 million in 1991, sales have grown by 50% each year since. The company attributes its success to understanding consumers' needs and practising user-centred design.[90]

Conversations were structured around five topics: healthcare, the home, leisure, transport and money. The assembled experts put forward ideas to address four questions:

- What can be done using existing technology or adaptations to existing technology?
- Where could technology transfers work well?
- What new technology could be developed?
- What are the barriers currently preventing improvements being adopted?

The simple, practical ideas put forward include the following:

PUBLIC-HIRE SCOOTERS

Mobility scooters for hire could be dotted around urban areas, in a similar way to public-hire bicycles in London. This would allow people to use scooters as and when they needed them, without having to store them in their homes (which can be difficult due to their bulk).[92]

TV BUDDIES

For many, television can be a solitary activity but watching programmes with others can increase people's enjoyment of them. An interface that allows people in different places to watch TV together could help people keep in touch with friends and relatives around the country. It could work in a similar way to Skype; the majority of the TV screen would show the programme but in the corner there could be a video link to a friend's living room.

← A practical, age-friendly prototypical version of a traditional scooter allows different generations to enjoy the same activity (see p 116).

A KETTLE THAT MONITORS BLOOD PRESSURE

Maintaining a healthy blood pressure can drastically reduce the risk of a cardiovascular event such as a heart attack or stroke. Research from the US has found that individuals who regularly monitor their own blood pressure at home find it easier to reduce it; 72% of those engaged in home monitoring had their blood pressure under control, compared to 57% of those who had conventional care. Sensor pads could be fitted to the handle of a kettle to provide regular monitoring by taking people's blood pressure as they make their morning tea. The individual would simply have to grip the handle while the kettle is heating the water.

A WATER BOTTLE THAT PREVENTS DEHYDRATION

Older people are considered to be at particular risk of dehydration, which can lead to functional and long-term health problems. Research has shown that cognitive and physical issues start to rise when the body water reduces by as little as 1%. A 'smart' water bottle could help people stay hydrated by monitoring how much water an individual has consumed, and calculating roughly how much they should be drinking depending on factors such as the weather. In response to the measurements, the bottle would glow green, amber or red.

5.5 Summary

This chapter highlights several contrasts – the need to look back as well forwards, to work with end users and learn from experts, and to remember the simple pleasures and attributes of the natural world that will always be enjoyable, as well as being aware of the increasingly sophisticated systems, gadgets and devices that could bring life-changing, even life-lengthening, opportunities.

That technology has the potential to help older and disabled people retain greater independence is not in doubt, but it is also clear that we need to avoid creating a different kind of dependency – potentially one that carries greater risks.

Fundamentally, we need homes that make us feel good – irrespective of age, culture or wealth. A great deal of current research shows that daylight, space, places to harbour possessions and memories, companionship and access to the outdoors – are still enormously important to us, particularly in later life.

The challenge lies in finding the right balance, as a society and as individuals.

> The challenge lies in finding the right balance, as a society and as individuals.

6.0 Conclusion

In this closing chapter we reflect on where we are with our understanding of the housing needs and wants of older people and what we have learned in the course of writing this book. Things have undoubtedly moved on in the ten years since the first HAPPI report and design has played a very significant role. Even so, too few of us consciously think about how we want to live our ever-lengthening lives. When we do, far fewer of us actually do something about it. Why is it that we still find it much easier to advise our friends and family than to reason with ourselves?

There are many unanswered questions but the fact that questions are being asked – by our politicians, our institutions, academics and housing professionals, and all of us – is progress in itself. And answers are beginning to emerge; new approaches to health and social care, as well as housing, are likely to make the next decade even more interesting than the last.

If it was ever a worthy ambition to spend our whole life in one home, we now know better. The housing shortage and rising levels of under-occupancy have focused attention on the need to use existing housing stock more efficiently and to encourage a better fit between the home we find ourselves living in and the home we need. While Lifetime Homes may not, with hindsight, have been the ideal name, its underlying principles of accessibility and adaptability remain sound as long as we are open-minded about moving as our circumstances change.

Housing experts have long argued that every new home should embody greater choice and flexibility, particularly as the vast majority of existing homes are not age-friendly, and very few are wheelchair accessible. Our needs can change quite quickly; we all experience bouts of illness or incapacity and we all want the ability to welcome older and disabled friends and relatives into our homes. Home adaptations are often difficult to arrange, expensive and a compromise when completed.

It makes sense to avoid or minimise loadbearing internal partitions, make hallways and doorways wide enough for wheelchairs, provide level thresholds and level shower facilities. Most of this is obvious, and very simple to incorporate if factored in from the start, but it is still not routine practice. Most mainstream housing developers, including many housing associations, only provide Category 2 and 3 homes where required to do so by local plans.

Government policy lacks conviction and foresight. The Nationally Described Space Standard is designed to accommodate Category 2 features but this is also subject to need and viability testing. Space is the ultimate enabler but space standards need not mean bigger homes, particularly as average household size is reducing. There is an acute shortage of 'care-ready', accessible homes with fewer, but larger, rooms and adequate storage. Assistive technology requires little more than a centrally placed Wi-Fi router (hub) close to a switched mains socket, allowing a range of monitoring, detection or assistive devices to be installed when needed.

Despite the logic of designing for resilience, housing designers have possibly never been under more pressure to save space, cut corners, and design down to minimum standards. It affects every element; we take for granted that we will be expected to minimise the number of soil and vent pipes in a dwelling, while paradoxically believing it would be sensible to include extra drainage connections to allow future occupants to adapt their homes to suit their changing priorities.

The principle of mixed and balanced communities remains sound and implies the planned provision of a wide range of housing options at a very local level. The models discussed in Chapter 2.0 cater for different lifestyles and tenures; all would play a useful role in every neighbourhood. And the ability to find a suitable home in the immediate vicinity makes moving a much more attractive proposition for many.

Co-living arrangements seem particularly likely to gain popularity. Multigenerational living in purpose-built housing with distinct, but connected, domains would be ideal for some extended families. Choosing to live with friends is also beginning to feel a very natural instinct in later life – for single people and couples. Today's young people have to wait longer for a home of their own and many, perhaps even most, will have house-shared and lived in an apartment before.

> Choosing to live with friends is also beginning to feel a very natural instinct in later life – for single people and couples.

An important theme for the future will be widening housing choice, challenging institutional and corporate models of living through principles of social inclusion, reciprocity and inter-dependence. Co-housing communities, to take one example, represent a particularly 'age-friendly' model of living. Created and run by their residents, these communities reinforce age-friendly principles of empowerment and agency, enabling older people to determine the shape of where and how they live whilst combatting social isolation. At their best, they provide a vocabulary for housing design for older age as residences that combine the self-contained, personal and private with the communal and shared spaces of residents living and managing their community life together.

Dr Sophie Handler, Manchester City Council and University of Manchester, and Professor Chris Phillipson, University of Manchester.

The need to anticipate the future while addressing the present has always been a key part of the architect's role.

Cohousing has so far proved difficult to realise, but a more speculative co-living model – a large house or a small group of apartments, designated for over-55s and designed to include an element of shared living for groups of friends – could prove popular. A growing number of examples across Europe suggests that we are increasingly choosing to live with people with whom we share common values or experiences.

The crisis in social care, and the growing need for temporary 'step down' accommodation for older people who currently cannot be discharged from hospital because they are unable to manage at home, are other imperatives. Currently, around 8,500 acute hospital beds per day are occupied by people who are ready to leave hospital in medical terms but are unable to do because their homes are unsuitable or they lack support. Delayed discharges harm the well-being of patients and their families, and are estimated to cost the NHS £820 million a year.[93]

The need to anticipate the future while addressing the present has always been a key part of the architect's role. It is difficult to judge whether the introduction of robotic carers will mean we need more private space or less. We may have to trust that much of today's best practice will still work tomorrow – but perhaps in a different way.

Most of the case studies that follow include home-grown examples of age-friendly housing that are at least as good as those we saw in Europe during the HAPPI visits of 2009. If today's best practice became tomorrow's normal, and the rate of delivery increased significantly, we would be much better equipped to deal with the future. But, in this final Viewpoint, Professor Myerson throws down the gauntlet and suggests there is some way to go.

VIEWPOINT | Jeremy Myerson: Are designers ready for ageing?

There is an inescapable mismatch in the UK between the profound and entirely predictable effects of demographic change on our future communities, neighbourhoods and homes, and current responses to designing for an ageing population, which tend to be shallow and uneven.

A demographic shift towards a society in which there are large numbers of older people and decreasing numbers of young people offers both challenges and opportunities for the design professions – but the question persists: are designers ready for ageing?

Across Europe, half the population will be over 50 by 2020. In the UK, 70% of population growth over the next 25 years will be in the over-60 age group and it is predicted that half of all children born today will live to be 103. Our life expectancy at birth has increased by five years in the past 20, so more years are a given for most us.

This longer lifespan is the direct result of such factors as falling mortality rates, better diet and advances in medical science, and should be something to celebrate. Instead we persist in seeing population ageing as a demographic time bomb, a disaster waiting to happen.

When it comes to housing, older people are seen as clogging up the market, occupying family homes for far longer than they should and failing to maintain them properly. This view is mirrored every year in winter, at a time of annual crisis in Britain's overflowing hospitals, when the headlines are all about elderly people clogging up the care system.

These negative narratives around ageing are familiar, but mask a more complicated picture. The old often hang on living in dilapidated family houses simply because of a lack of smaller alternatives that are fit for purpose and have two bedrooms, and because the upkeep and future-proofing of domestic property is so difficult to achieve.

A wider question is how we will live those extra years most of us are now granted. Will we enjoy independence and a good quality of life? Or will we become isolated and marginalised? The debate can be crystallised in the phrase 'years full of life – or life full of years?'

Housing design is central to this debate. Design generally has a critical role to play in how successfully we will age: it affects how we build our homes and neighbourhoods, how we work and travel, and what products and services we will use in the future. Well-designed homes are pivotal to such issues as care, health, work and social interaction.

What holds back architects and designers in the UK from engaging more whole-heartedly with this important field? I believe that the big obstacle is not technical – it is cultural. There remain deep-rooted stereotypes around ageing which have diverted the attention of an architectural community much more comfortable focusing on younger or family-formation building users. The stigma of growing old persists and this needs to be challenged if designers are to be ready for demographic change.

In early 2017, I curated a short-run, pop-up exhibition at the Design Museum in London called 'NEW OLD: Designing For Our Future Selves', prior to an international tour. The purpose of the show was to demonstrate how design could enhance later life, helping people to lead fuller, richer, healthier lives right into old age. At the heart of the exhibition were six specially commissioned projects to explore the potential of new design for the old.

Alongside outdoor furniture to help older people announce their place in the working world rather than retreat from view, a new-look mobility scooter to help a grandmother interact on the same terms as with her micro scooter-riding grandchild, and an AI (Artificial Intelligence) -powered undergarment to assist with basic muscle movement, there were inevitably projects about housing.

One speculative project by Future Facility, called 'Amazin Apartments', advanced the idea of a modular stress- and maintenance-free apartment for the elderly serviced from hidden corridors by a technology company. In this scenario, the fridge is restocked, clothes washed, lights changed and temperature controlled without a human being ever entering the home, with data from millions of older users collected, aggregated and analysed to optimise all the unseen, tech-driven input.

If the Amazin Apartments project turned residents into passive, comfortable and well-served prisoners in their own homes (no need to pop down to the local shops for a pint of milk), then another project – Hemingway Design's Staiths South Bank housing estate in Gateshead – took the opposite tack. This made a design virtue of taking older people out of their own homes to interact with neighbours via outdoor communal barbecue stations and table tennis tables.

Between these two extremes, there is a wealth of opportunity in housing design for older people. It is conventional to see a spectrum, from well-established physical design strategies that encourage social interaction to new virtual technologies that can replace human contact with robots, big data and AI. However, the future is likely to feature a combination of both types of intervention.

Whatever way our future homes take shape, it would be advisable for architects and designers to try to think beyond a medical model of ageing that views growing older as a disease to be cured and is primarily about dependency, decrepitude and death. The medical model of ageing is why we have so many designs for older people that either belong in a hospital or look like a hospital. We can all think of aids and appliances that try to help but end up stigmatising the user.

We need to think differently about ageing and view growing older less in terms of addressing medical deficits and more in terms of supporting a social model of ageing (productive new connections and aspirations in later life) and even a cultural model of ageing (this period of life is so unique and special that it demands particular cultural and creative attention). This is because future cohorts will work, travel, contribute and crave new experiences and relationships for longer than any before in human history.

Getting older is a natural part of life that will happen to all of us. As we head deep into the century of the centenarian, we must stop being in a kind of design denial. The demographic realities of ageing populations combined with the inadequacies of our housing stock demand that we try something new.

Jeremy Myerson, Helen Hamlyn Professor of Design at the Royal College of Art and a Visiting Fellow at the Oxford Institute of Population Ageing, University of Oxford. He is the curator of the Design Museum's exhibition, NEW OLD: Designing for Our Future Selves.

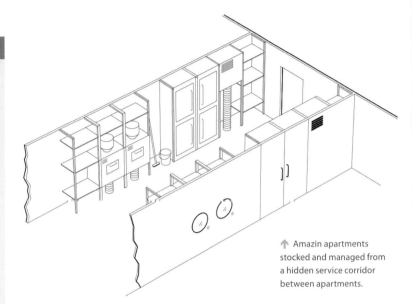

↑ Amazin apartments stocked and managed from a hidden service corridor between apartments.

Myerson's message is pertinent not only to designers, but to everyone. It is salutary that almshouses, many of which are centuries old, remain so popular today. Despite their practical shortcomings, these well-built, characterful buildings still demonstrate that their occupants are a valued part of the community. It is telling that most of the sheltered housing built in the second half of the last century has had nothing like the same enduring appeal.

As we consider the future design of age-friendly housing, success will lie in remembering the simple, the practical and the humane, as we also imagine radically different ways of living that embrace the best of technology. Remaining connected – to places and people – via personal contact and through various forms of technology-enabled virtual realities – is a recurring theme. It is clear that well-designed, flexible and sustainable housing that values and appeals to older people ultimately benefits everyone.

↑ Seismic Powered Suit by fuseproject helps with muscle movement.

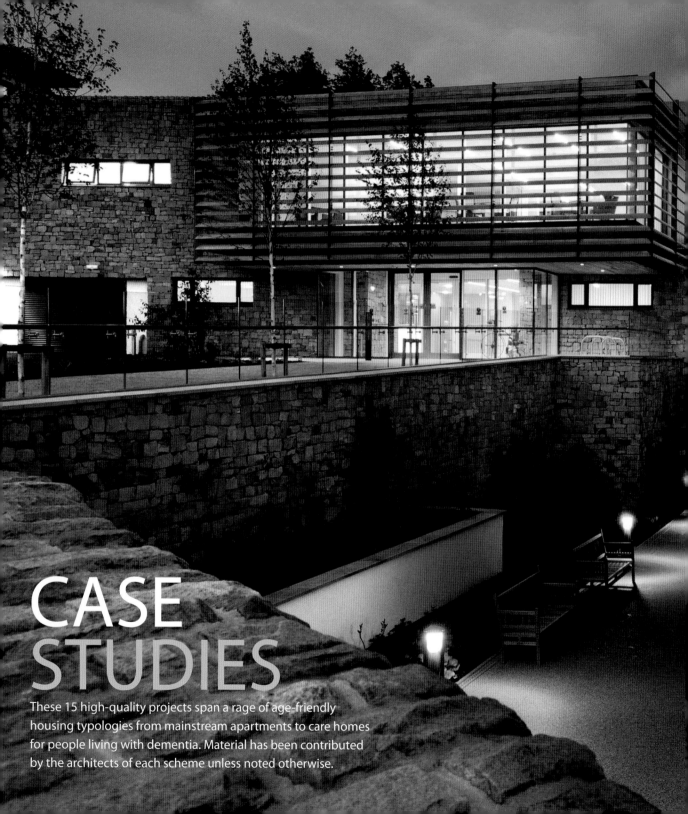

CASE STUDIES

These 15 high-quality projects span a rage of age-friendly housing typologies from mainstream apartments to care homes for people living with dementia. Material has been contributed by the architects of each scheme unless noted otherwise.

CASE STUDY 1

Parkside

DEVELOPMENT TYPE: Mixed use (mainstream housing and commercial)

LOCATION: Matlock, Derbyshire

CLIENT: Barncroft Homes

ARCHITECT: Evans Vettori

CONTRACTOR: Barncroft Homes

CONSTRUCTION VALUE: £1.8m

COMPLETION DATE: July 2014

NUMBER OF HOMES: 10 apartments, 4 retail units

TENURE MIX: 100% outright sale

AGE RANGE: 'Retirement age' (self-selecting)

> *Perhaps it is because these apartments were not designed with a stereotype in mind that they are so successful, naturally avoiding any sense of 'ageism'.*

CONCEPT/RATIONALE

Although not originally designed for a particular demographic, this mixed-use redevelopment of a former hotel car park, in the Derbyshire spa town of Matlock, has been a huge success with 'downsizers'.

Barncroft Homes purchased the brownfield site with a view to maximising profit, so budget and value for money were key drivers. However, the director recognised the importance of this historic town centre site and was committed to a sensitive development embedded in his own community.

Parkside is located on an active pedestrian route that cuts through the busy town centre giving convenient access to local shops and a footbridge across the river to the nearby Hall Leys Park. Through collaboration with the local planning authority (Derbyshire Dales District Council) and their conservation team, ten two-bedroom apartments were designed to sit over four ground floor retail units.

The location has played a large part in attracting the retired couples who now live here. Local shops and amenities are within easy walking distance as are local transport links; the apartments each have a parking space too. One of the new retail units in the development is now a busy cafe and another has been let to a hairdresser; perfectly located for the residents of Parkside.

The street-level arcade reduces the massing of the building and animates the street scene. As well as providing a more comfortable threshold in inclement weather and a meeting place for shoppers, it allows the cafe to spill out – animating the space further and encouraging social interaction.

←←← Ground floor plan.

←← Simple, bold elevational treatment.

← Typical upper floor plan.

↓ Light-filled apartment.

POINTS OF SPECIAL INTEREST

The design of the light, spacious apartments appealed to the older generation. They also have low on-going energy costs. U-values are 20% better than regulations require and masonry walls provide high thermal mass to absorb and retain heat. High-performance windows and doors contribute further to the thermal performance, and the comfort of residents.

The apartments have 'outdoor rooms', as opposed to gardens or balconies. These spaces are large enough to accommodate a table and chairs outside and create pockets of 'garden'; several are located on corners to increase daylight.

The scheme has step-free access throughout, and bathrooms were modified to suit the particular needs of each prospective owner as they were identified. This tailored approach is another reason for the success of the scheme, which is managed by a resident-owned company. Perhaps it is the very fact that these apartments were not designed with a stereotype in mind that they are so successful, naturally avoiding any sense of 'ageism'.

TESTIMONIAL

'Overall, the DWELL participants who visited Parkside really enjoyed the scheme, with one commenting that it had renewed her faith in apartment living! Many of the strengths of Parkside lie in some of the finer details – the way the scheme has been planned, designed, detailed, marketed, and sold – and the way that the ongoing building management is organised'.

DR ADAM PARK (from the DWELL project)

'We loved it because of the light all the way around. It's just absolutely great'.

PARKSIDE RESIDENT

CASE STUDY 2

Castlemaine Court

DEVELOPMENT TYPE: Multigenerational housing

LOCATION: Rectory Lane, Byfleet, Surrey

CLIENT: Crown Simmons Housing

ARCHITECT: Archadia Architects

CONTRACTOR: William Lacey Group

CONSTRUCTION VALUE: £2.1m

COMPLETION DATE: August 2014

NUMBER OF HOMES: 16 apartments
(4 x 1 bed, 12 x 2 bed)

TENURE MIX: 100% affordable

AGE RANGE: 0–60+

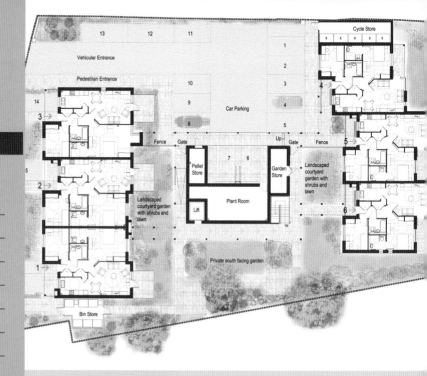

CONCEPT/RATIONALE

Castlemaine Court replaces a sheltered block of low-demand bedsit accommodation for older people. Originally intended to be for over-55s, the local authority wanted the scheme to become multigenerational in order to accommodate some young families and other households who were desperately in need of affordable housing.

The importance of affordability was highlighted in the Council's Strategic Market Housing Assessment, and Crown Simmons Housing responded to this by utilising recycled grant and reserves to build a new scheme that could be let at 'social rent' levels (on average 40% of the market rent for the area).

Although designed on a tight budget, the completed development is suitable for all generations and incorporates HAPPI recommendations to allow people to remain in their own homes into old age. Collaboration was crucial, and a public consultation enabled the local community to be involved throughout the planning process with an emphasis on genuine empowerment. A local councillor became an important link between the design team and the local community.

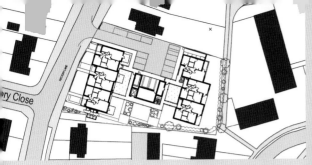

← ← Ground floor plan.

← Site plan.

↙ Upper floor plan.

↓ The central three storey block with connecting decks.

POINTS OF SPECIAL INTEREST

The success of this scheme lies in the sense of community engendered by the design. Dual aspect apartments open onto walkways, enabling a single staircase to serve the entire development and avoiding the long, dark corridors and escape stairs needed in more traditional, enclosed layouts. There is lift access to the upper floors and walk-in showers in all apartments. The design of the apartments allows single people, couples and families to be housed as one community, and door widths and circulation spaces facilitate wheelchair access throughout.

The walkways are an integral part of the building; not an 'add-on'. Over-sailing roofs help to define areas in front of the first floor apartments, creating a generous semi-private forecourt to each home. By eliminating corridors, the walkways also increase the natural light and ventilation to the apartments.

To reduce its bulk, the building is split into three blocks, each of which has a reason for its location. The scale and massing respond to the surrounding buildings, with two-storey blocks located to the rear of the site and fronting Rectory Lane, to continue the existing street pattern. Ground floor entrance doors in the latter block face onto the street, while the upper apartments look into the site, giving this terrace the

appearance of three separate houses. These mask the central block, enabling it to be three storeys to increase the total number of homes. A communal biomass boiler burns sustainable wooden pellets to provide heating and hot water.

The scheme was delivered using a partnering contract, which allowed a collaborative approach during the construction process. As part of a value-engineering exercise, significant cost savings were made by a thorough investigation of the materials proposed for the walkways.

Revisiting the scheme, Archadia has learned that residents use the walkways as an extension of the home; sitting out on them in the summer, interacting with neighbours and looking out onto the communal gardens, which are also well-used. The sense of collective ownership is evident in the way residents have clubbed together to buy shared garden furniture and been involved in communal activities such as a sunflower growing competition, for which Crown Simmons Housing provided a prize.

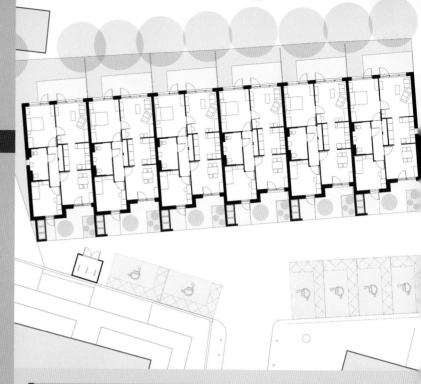

CASE STUDY 3

Greenwich Housing

DEVELOPMENT TYPE: Bungalows for older people

LOCATION: Greenwich, London

CLIENT: Royal Borough of Greenwich

ARCHITECT: Bell Phillips Architects

CONTRACTOR: Newlyns

CONSTRUCTION VALUE: £4.3m

COMPLETION DATE: September 2015

NUMBER OF HOMES: 22 homes across five sites

TENURE MIX: 100% affordable rent

AGE RANGE: 55+

▌ CONCEPT/RATIONALE

The Royal Borough of Greenwich approached Bell Phillips Architects to consider new housing developments on six semi-derelict, garage sites owned by the council. The council also identified that many of its retirement-age tenants were under-occupying large houses, and research had suggested that many would like to move to single-storey dwellings. With this in mind, the architects were asked to design bungalows, releasing large houses for new families who desperately needed them, and resolving problematic garage sites that were attracting anti-social behaviour and were a blight on their respective neighbourhoods.

The architects developed a single bungalow typology that could be used on every site to make construction more affordable. This was challenging because each site had a different orientation and the neighbouring buildings varied in scale. In all cases, it was difficult to imagine how a single-storey dwelling could be appropriate alongside Victorian terraced houses of two or more storeys. In addition, many of the sites were compact and required the new homes to be built very close to the street edge, with virtually no threshold between the home and the pavement, and the risk that they would lack privacy.

With these two issues in mind, a design was developed with a very large, dormer, clerestory window, which pops up above the roofline. This increases the scale and

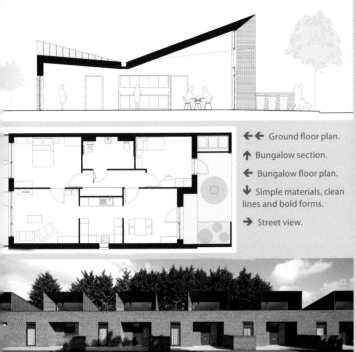

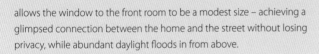

←← Ground floor plan.

↑ Bungalow section.

← Bungalow floor plan.

↓ Simple materials, clean lines and bold forms.

→ Street view.

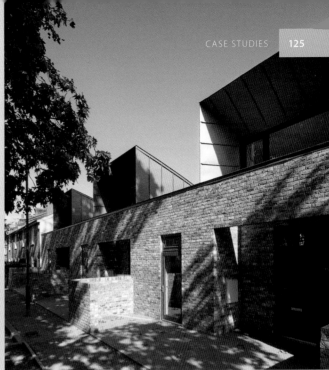

allows the window to the front room to be a modest size – achieving a glimpsed connection between the home and the street without losing privacy, while abundant daylight floods in from above.

The open plan living/dining/kitchen arrangement was an important response to the changing patterns of 21st century living. The space is double-height below the clerestory at the front, descending to a standard height ceiling at the centre of the plan where the kitchen is located, and rising again where the living room opens to the garden at the rear. Although the dining space was notionally planned at the front, and living at the rear, the flexible plan allows occupants to swap dining and living if they wish.

> *Conversations with new residents have confirmed that people are overjoyed, largely due to the sense of wellbeing gained from the bright and spacious interiors.*

POINTS OF SPECIAL INTEREST

The homes have two bedrooms and an internal floor area of $89m^2$. The principal bedroom is at the rear, opening to the privacy of the small garden. The second bedroom is at the front; it can be used as a study or hobbies room, a spare bedroom for grandchildren, visitors, or live-in carer. There is ample storage and a large bathroom.

All homes are timber framed with brick cladding and a zinc standing seam roof, detailed to give sharp edges around the clerestory. This was not simple to achieve and the roofing subcontractor must be applauded for the effort spent in achieving such a neat finish. Designed to Code for Sustainable Homes Level 4, they should stay cool in our increasingly hot summers as well as retaining heat in winter. The living room doors can be opened to the garden and the clerestory windows opened to the street, allowing cross-ventilation without compromising security, even at night.

The tall internal spaces and abundant daylight from the clerestory make these homes a pleasure to live in. Conversations with new residents have confirmed that people are overjoyed, largely due to the sense of wellbeing gained from the bright and spacious interiors.

CASE STUDY 4

New Ground

DEVELOPMENT TYPE: Cohousing for older women

LOCATION: High Barnet, London

CLIENT: Older Women's Cohousing (OWCH) and Hanover Housing Association

ARCHITECT: Pollard Thomas Edwards (PTE)

CONTRACTOR: Quinn London Limited

CONSTRUCTION VALUE: £4.7m

COMPLETION DATE: December 2016

NUMBER OF HOMES: 25 apartments
(11 x 1 bed, 11 x 2 bed, 3 x 3 bed)

TENURE MIX: 17 private sale, 8 affordable rent

AGE RANGE: 51–87

> *… It soon became clear that the single entrance and lift core presented an opportunity for social interaction. While developer-led housing minimises circulation to maximise net residential (saleable) floor space, OWCH placed social value in the generosity of these 'in-between spaces'.*

CONCEPT/RATIONALE

New Ground is the first senior cohousing project in the UK. It creates 25 bespoke homes and several shared spaces, including a common room, that establish a sense of group identity and community. The common room and the majority of homes are arranged around a shared 'secret garden'.

OWCH have been working together for many years, pioneering the idea of an intentional, mutually supportive community for women in later life. From the start, their ambition was to take ownership of their older age and to develop a cohousing community, whose residents would play a meaningful role in its design, benefit from the mutual support of neighbours, feel part of a community and remain active.

Building on their role in the 2009 HAPPI report, PTE were appointed in 2010, by not-for-profit retirement housing provider Hanover, to collaborate with OWCH on the design of their ideal community on a site in the Wood Street Conservation Area in Barnet. They developed a series of collaborative design workshops for OWCH and other stakeholders to develop the design of the site layout, communal areas, materials and appearance and the design of individual homes. Sessions were geared to giving the group the tools to discuss questions such as: 'How should this ideal community be laid out?', 'What's the route to my flat and the view from it?', 'Where are the shared spaces and what will they be used for?' Many of the ideas expressed shaped the finished building and these nuances in the design together express the innovations of OWCH.

> *Cohousing is all about creating communities which are responsible for themselves. Being so involved in the initial stages of planning our project has been a hugely important part of achieving these aims.*

←← Site plan.

↑ Apartments provide a neutral background for personalisation.

← The official launch.

→ Homes look out onto the shared garden.

POINTS OF SPECIAL INTEREST

A key consensus that emerged from the collaborative process was the idea that homes would as far as possible be united by a common outlook over a shared garden. This is manifest in the finished building, and the courtyard arrangement sends a powerful message about how the group want to live together and individually. Other key aspects were the desire for a single entrance and for the common room to sit adjacent to this, at the heart of the community.

The idea of collective identity carries through not only in the way homes are configured but also in how they appear. Early on in the collaborative process the idea of a collection of 'little houses' emerged. Within this idea there was an aspiration for domesticity, as well an understanding that each element would need to respond to its setting within the site. The entrance falls between the 'little houses', with exposed brick faces marking their edges. The 'little houses' to the north define a street frontage and provide a contemporary response to the Union Street vernacular, while the garden apartments relate to the more industrial buildings to the rear of the High Street. The brick and dark grey metalwork unify the various elements.

It soon became clear that the single entrance and lift core presented an opportunity for social interaction. While developer-led housing minimises circulation to maximise net residential (saleable) floor space, OWCH placed social value in the generosity of these 'in-between spaces'.

TESTIMONIAL

'Taking part in workshops arranged by PTE, in which we worked on the basic design of our cohousing complex, was a huge learning curve for all of the Older Women's Co-Housing group – and an enormously satisfying one.

First of all it helped each of us clarify our ideas of what exactly it was we wanted from cohousing and to understand the limitations that cost, practicability, planning considerations and the site itself imposed on our ideals.

Secondly, our discussions on these topics, and the undertaking of such practical exercises as drawing what we had in mind and finding pictures of buildings we liked, were an extremely effective way of getting each of us to feel that we owned the project, and that what would be produced in the end would be uniquely ours. Thirdly, the whole process was an excellent way of getting us to understand each other better and to bond as a group. Cohousing is all about creating communities which are responsible for themselves. Being so involved in the initial stages planning our project has been a hugely important part of achieving these aims.'

RACHEL, A RESIDENT OF NEW GROUND

CASE STUDY 5

Kotisatama

DEVELOPMENT TYPE: Cohousing for seniors

LOCATION: Helsinki, Finland

CLIENT: Aktiiviset Seniorit ry (Active Seniors Association)

ARCHITECT: Kirsti Sivén & Asko Takala Architects (in collaboration with the residents)

CONTRACTOR: YIT Rakennus Oy

CONSTRUCTION VALUE: €16,135,000

COMPLETION DATE: June 2015

NUMBER OF HOMES: 22 x 2-room apartments, 34 x larger apartments and 63 studios

TENURE MIX: 100% outright sale[i]

AGE RANGE: 52–81 (official minimum age of 48)

CONCEPT/RATIONALE

The Active Seniors Association was founded by a group of people looking for an active and communal way of living, which they could not find in the Finnish market. They had seen for themselves the difficulty of arranging care for their relatives and wanted to take this into their own hands.

Kirsti Sivén was involved at a very early stage as the architects have studied alternative housing solutions for years. The cohousing vision has driven the project; future residents get to know each other, evaluate needs and values (and costs). They find the plot, choose the architect and share the design process.

In addition to co-designing their own flats, the residents of Kotisatama played an important part in designing the common areas. These include a community kitchen, dining room, library, small sitting area, office, bike store and shared laundry, on the ground/first floor, and saunas, exercise room, multipurpose sitting room with fireplace and roof garden, on the top floor.

The community enjoys a lively and varied social life. Everybody is required to look after the common areas; only technical maintenance is trusted to an outsider. A shared meal is served from Monday to Friday at 5pm, except for the summer months. Cooking together and sharing the meals are the most important and popular events, well-liked by those who are 'on duty' and those who enjoy the outcome. The week long turn of each group of 12–13 residents comes every six weeks.

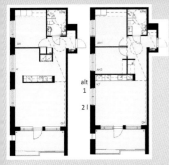

← ← Site plan.

↑ Library.

← A choice of apartment layout.

→ Large balconies accessed via glazed, sliding extend panels extend private living space.

POINTS OF SPECIAL INTEREST

The first senior cohousing project of the office was Loppukiri (The Final Spurt). The co-design process allows future residents to get involved and make choices through searching discussion with the architects. In Kotisatama, the shared facilities were designed with thematic residents' working groups, and discussed and decided in community meetings.

The apartment design began by studying the needs and hopes of the future residents: size, layout, room division, location and so on. The architects' design package included two or three sessions with each resident; using sketches, the first focused on spatial choices, the others on fixtures and finishing. Each step was documented and confirmed later, and extra consultation was available at additional cost. In late 2017, of the 85 residents in total, there were 20 couples, 42 single females and three single males.

The street-level, double-height dining room, located on the street corner, is also used for events and a hobbies room. Instead of the tiny domestic saunas that are now common in Finnish owner-occupied housing, Kotisatama has two sauna-units on the top floor, along with the other recreational facilities, which include a roof garden with space for container planting.

The architects take a very broad view of sustainability and consider the 'Design for All' philosophy to be crucial. The shared spaces promote sociability and wellbeing, are energy- and resource-efficient, and easy to maintain. This brings economic benefits too. The large balconies have glazed, sliding panels to extend their use.

Kotisatama is located in the new Kalasatama district. The Smart Kalasatama project is an experimental innovation platform to cocreate smart infrastructure and services. The Kotisatama community uses these services in many ways; for example info-screens in the lobby show the next public transport connections and residents can reserve sauna and laundry sessions online. The other half of the block, Leonsatama Housing, is ordinary owner-occupied senior housing for over-55s by ATT, Helsinki Housing Production.

NOTE

[1] Hitas is a housing price-and-quality control system used in Helsinki on city-owned leased land sites. It is aimed at ensuring that housing prices are based on real production costs. The maximum prices of both new and old Hitas units are regulated. The Hitas register and the resale is managed by the City of Helsinki.

CASE STUDY 6

Chapter House

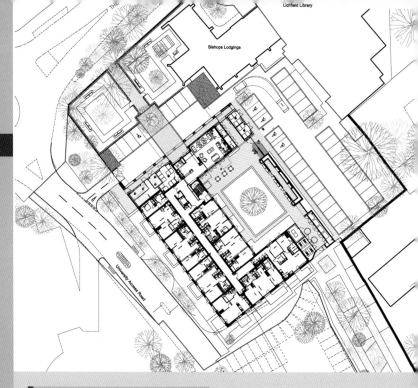

DEVELOPMENT TYPE: Later living apartments

LOCATION: Lichfield, Staffordshire

CLIENT: PegasusLife

ARCHITECT: Proctor and Matthews Architects

CONTRACTOR: Gr8 Space Ltd

CONSTRUCTION VALUE: £6.3m

COMPLETION DATE: April 2017

NUMBER OF HOMES: 38 apartments
(12 x 1 bed, 26 x 2 bed)

TENURE MIX: 100% private

AVERAGE AGE OF RESIDENTS: 55+

CONCEPT/RATIONALE

Located within Lichfield's Central Conservation Area, the design for Chapter House retirement/later living community draws inspiration from the characteristic historic morphology of Lichfield's walled gardens and the original cloistered form of the demolished medieval friary, which once occupied the site.

Remnants of these ancient walled structures remain. The distinctive gables and chimneys of the Bishop's Lodging and a linear walled garden known locally as the Monk's Walk, which is publically accessible and maintained by local residents, provide key markers within the site. These establish the armature around which a series of new public and communal pathways, gardens, cloisters and courtyards are created. This provides the external spaces for neighbourly interaction and community activity, and a visual focus for the 38 one and two bedroom later living apartments within the development.

A publically accessible route connects a new pocket park on the principal frontage to the building via a cloistered frontage to the central courtyard. This garden court is framed by a linear orangery/conservatory (with echoes of the historic garden form of Lichfield). This helps to define the edge to the central space and provides a buffer between the tranquil garden and the adjacent walled parking court, located to the rear of the adjacent public library. The route continues beneath the new building, passing a newly created garden equipment store (provided for local amenity groups) before arriving at the Monk's Walk public garden. This sequence will provide visible daily activity within the development and help to integrate new residents closely within the existing community.

←← Ground floor plan.

← View from Monk's Walk to central courtyard.

↙ Entrance to Monk's Walk from entrance cloister.

↓ Entrance facade and cloister.

POINTS OF SPECIAL INTEREST

Chapter House incorporates a number of internal and external facilities that will encourage neighbourly interaction between new residents and locals, nurturing a sense of community and security within the development. The sequence of spaces around the building (including the incorporation of the existing Monk's Walk landscaped garden) helps to create a safe and leisurely 'exercise' circuit for older residents.

A large residents' lounge, self-service 'honesty bar' and relaxed kitchen area occupy the space between the arrival cloister and associated pocket park, and the more tranquil, sun-filled communal courtyard garden in the centre of the development. Floor to ceiling glazing on both principal facades maximises natural light and creates a seamless visual link to the entrance, new pocket park and the focal landscaped courtyard. Glazed doors open out to a south-facing sheltered seating area within the central court to enable residents to socialise in the summer sun. A dual-facing central hearth and fireplace is located between the entrance reception hall and communal lounge, providing a warm and cosy focus for the winter months.

Covered, communal south-facing balconies are located at first- and second-floor levels in a staggered arrangement to avoid over-shadowing. This will also enable less mobile residents to interact with neighbours on all floors without the need to venture far from their individual apartments.

A linear orangery/conservatory defines the eastern edge of the central walled courtyard garden, providing a tempered, sheltered environment for residents and an opportunity to engage in gardening activities. Importantly, this not only extends seasonal use, but also provides a space in which residents can engage with the local community groups that currently maintain the existing Monk's Walk garden. A small apartment for visiting relatives or friends is located on the ground floor.

Careful attention has been given to the texture and materiality of the buildings. The entrance cloister is lined with vertical oak boarding to provide a warm, high-quality threshold to the development. The upper storeys offer deep reveals to windows set within thick textured brickwork walls, implying protection. The distinctive vertically ribbed, 'corduroy' brickwork (a mixture of red and Staffordshire blue bricks) to the upper floors is configured to visually mitigate the height of the building; again providing warmth and texture. White bricks within the central court bounce light around the space, helping to create a bright and inviting landscaped focus at the heart of the development.

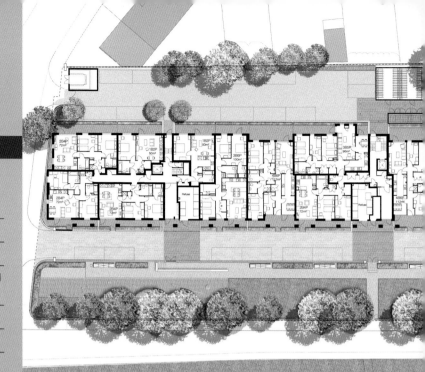

CASE STUDY 7

Lime Tree Court (formerly Buccleuch House)

DEVELOPMENT TYPE: Multigenerational housing

LOCATION: Clapton Common, London

CLIENT: Hanover Housing Association, Agudas Israel Housing Association (AIHA) and Hill

ARCHITECT: Levitt Bernstein

CONTRACTOR: Hill

CONSTRUCTION VALUE: £15m

COMPLETION DATE: 2015

NUMBER OF HOMES: 107, comprising:

- 41 assisted living apartments for older people (Hanover)
- 28 affordable rent and shared ownership apartments for the local Orthodox Jewish population (Agudas Israel Housing Association)
- 38 private sale apartments (Hill)

AGE RANGE: 55+ for Hanover element

CONCEPT/RATIONALE

This unusual project had three separate clients, each with a distinct brief for a particular type of housing. Hanover sought to provide affordable rented one and two bedroom apartments and supporting communal space for older people; AIHA were looking for mainly larger family homes for the local Orthodox Jewish community; and Hill, a mix of one and two bedroom apartments for first-time buyers and young families.

The long, shallow site flanks Clapton Common. This had two main design implications; first, that the three types of housing, each with its own entrance and circulation core, could only sit side by side; second, that the need for outdoor communal space was reduced because of the proximity of the park.

> This cross-generational scheme triumphs because it offers a broad spectrum of housing within a single block, while respecting the needs of very different user groups.
>
> RICHARD BLAKEWAY,
> FORMER DEPUTY MAYOR OF LONDON

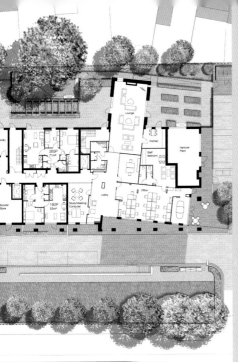

← ← Ground floor plan (assisted living on the right).

← Canopied balconies to apartments for Orthodox Jewish families.

↙ View from Clapton Common.

↓ Flexible 'HAPPI apartment'.

POINTS OF SPECIAL INTEREST

Despite the three different types of accommodation, the building reads as one. Closer inspection of the facade reveals subtle differences in the fenestration and balconies of the three constituent parts, practical responses to the needs of each user group:

- The private apartments for Hill are open plan but designed to be able to adapt to Orthodox Jewish requirements should that be useful when they are sold on. They have simple, stacking, cantilevered balconies.

- The majority of homes for the Orthodox Jewish families have three or more bedrooms. In order to meet AIHA's specific requirements, which include extra sinks and external storage needed during religious festivals, they are 10% larger than the GLA standards. Balconies are staggered to provide a clear view of the sky when converted into sukkahs during the Sukkot festival when they are often used for sleeping, eating and entertaining.

- The Hanover extra care apartments have glazed winter gardens to provide more shelter than conventional balconies and create extra year-round 'living space'. Sliding glass panels allow them to be enclosed in colder weather to provide a protected 'conservatory', and opened up on warmer days to form a semi-open balcony.

The assisted living element has a lively, double-height reception area with glimpses of the communal spaces beyond. A secondary entrance bypasses these more public areas and leads directly up to the residential storeys – giving residents the choice to come and go discretely, or seek company as they do so. Adopting the principle of progressive privacy, the building becomes more private and more secure the deeper and higher you go.

Communal spaces include a large, ground-floor lounge, smaller double-height sitting spaces on alternate floors, two enclosed rear gardens and a roof terrace. One garden, a peaceful sunken courtyard, features sensory planting, pergolas and seating areas for quiet respite, and the other, a kitchen garden, has raised beds for food growing.

All apartments are at least 10% larger than GLA minima, and accommodate wheelchair users. Though Hanover has standard apartment plans, they were keen to trial some more flexible 'HAPPI style' semi-open plan layouts with a sliding partition between the living space and the bedroom.

Lime Tree Court is now home to a multicultural, mixed-age community. Its architectural and social strengths lie in the ease with which it accommodates diversity without prioritising or disadvantaging any group of residents.

CASE STUDY 8

Heald Farm Court

DEVELOPMENT TYPE: Extra care and community hub

LOCATION: Earlestown, Newton-le-Willows, St Helens, Merseyside

CLIENT: Helena Partnerships

ARCHITECT: DK-Architects

CONTRACTOR: Cruden Construction Ltd

CONSTRUCTION VALUE: £10.6m

COMPLETION DATE: September 2009

NUMBER OF HOMES: 86 x 2 bed apartments, 3 x 2 bed bungalows

TENURE MIX: 50% social rent, 25% sale, 25% shared ownership

AGE RANGE: 55+

CONCEPT/RATIONALE

In December 2004, St Helens Metropolitan Borough Council made strategic decisions on the future of its 'Elderly Persons Homes', with the aim of improving the range of housing and care options for its increasingly ageing population. Following extensive consultation, it was agreed that two of the homes would be developed as support centres for older people, and the rest decommissioned over time and the sites redeveloped to provide extra care housing.

Heald Farm Court replaced an existing 40-bed residential care facility with an extra care scheme providing 89 apartments/bungalows and an extensive range of on-site and outreach services for older and more vulnerable people. The desired outcomes were:

- Wider tenure choice for older people
- Additional layers of intermediate care at home
- Increased use of assistive technology
- Reduced dependence on residential care
- Increased provision for people living with mental health problems
- Fewer in-hospital bed days and emergency bed days
- Fewer unplanned admissions to hospital
- Fewer hospital re-admissions
- Opportunities for more intensive care management
- Fewer falls
- Greater promotion of healthy lifestyles
- Greater community sustainability.

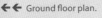 ← ← Ground floor plan.

← The popular hub anchors the development in the local community.

⬉ ⬇ Simple forms of a domestic scale and robust materials.

POINTS OF SPECIAL INTEREST

St Helens Metropolitan Borough Council set out to achieve a high-quality development by gifting the land to the developer, Helena Partnerships, and working up the design with the developer, healthcare provider (MHA) and the architects. The extensive communal facilities are intended to serve as a village hub for another 166 homes in the surrounding area, including new bungalows developed simultaneously on a separate site.

The layout therefore has to work for three distinct users: the visitor must feel welcome, the self-reliant resident should not feel institutionalised, and the more dependent should feel secure. The design achieves this by dividing apartments into three blocks enveloping a services hub.

The most independent residents live in the street frontage block along Sturgess Street and access the hub via a covered walkway. Frailer residents can access the services without going outdoors. The two routes for visitors to the hub (one pedestrian and one vehicular) converge at the concierge desk. Once signed in, visitors have access to a range of dining, leisure and healthcare facilities. Although these are intended for those in retirement, no-one is turned away; MHA reports that the hub has become the area's liveliest venue with activities drawing in some people in their 40s.

Apartments have a generous living space, a large double bedroom and a single bedroom, which can also be used as a study or, in some cases, opened up to the living area. This provides for a variety of living arrangements including single or double occupancy, and sleepovers by family or carers. The apartments can be adapted to meet future needs – bathrooms have level-access showers, and are connected to bedrooms, allowing hoist transfer if required. Ground floor homes have their own garden area and those on upper floors have balconies.

The central spaces are similarly flexible; the lounge and dining areas are a series of interconnected spaces capable of adaptation for different uses throughout the day, and over the life of the building.

> ❝ … the hub has become the area's liveliest venue with activities drawing in some people in their 40s.

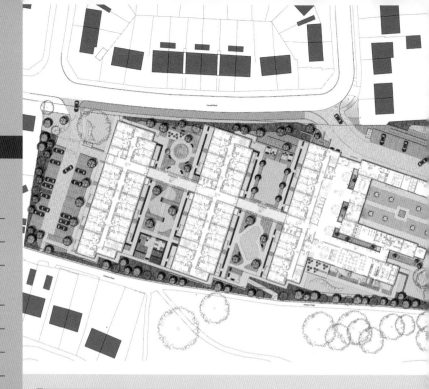

CASE STUDY 9

Willow Barns

DEVELOPMENT TYPE: Extra care

LOCATION: Blurton, Stoke-on-Trent

CLIENT: The Sapphire Consortium, including Kajima UK, the Eric Wright Group and Your Housing Group

ARCHITECT: PRP

CONTRACTOR: Eric Wright Construction

CONSTRUCTION VALUE: £14.5m

COMPLETION DATE: May 2016

NUMBER OF HOMES: 75 apartments (27 x 1 bed plus, 48 x 2 bed)

TENURE MIX: 100% affordable rent

AVERAGE AGE OF TENANTS: 75+

CONCEPT/RATIONALE

Willow Barns is part of the local authority's wider vision to:

- Create a quality sustainable and personalised housing solution that enables older people to live in their own home for longer.
- Provide a supportive environment that promotes health and wellbeing, maximising opportunities for older people to maintain or regain independence while ensuring ready access to care and support, if and when required.
- Deliver a hub for older people in the surrounding neighbourhood to access high-quality day care, recreation and welfare support.
- Enable people with physical and mental health conditions to continue to participate and play an active role in their own community.

It forms part of an initiative to deliver specialist housing for older people across Stoke, which culminated in a Private Finance Initiative (PFI) project being brought to the market in 2012. Following a competitive dialogue process this was awarded to the Sapphire Consortium in 2014, and has now delivered 390 apartments across three sites. The two sister projects to Willow Barns are Oak Priory in Abbey Hulton, to the east of the city centre, and Maple West in Chell, to the north.

The vision for Willow Barns focused on the needs of both the residents and the wider Blurton community, contributing to the locality by enhancing the existing sense of place.

←← Ground floor plan.

← Inside the atrium.

→ The atrium at the entrance links the barn and the new building.

↙ Fully glazed walkways link residential wings and offer views across gardens and beyond.

↓ The facilities serve residents and the local community.

▌ POINTS OF SPECIAL INTEREST

The design was inspired by the early 19th century agricultural buildings on the site. While these are not listed, they make a valuable contribution to the character of the area. They were therefore retained, converted into communal areas for residents, and integrated with the new buildings. These locally important historic buildings now have a new positive use and make a major contribution to the sense of place generated by the development.

The main new build accommodation is within three structures, designed with a barn aesthetic. Aligned on a north–south axis, they step down the sloping site. They are linked at the first and second floors with dramatic fully glazed, bridge structures, which contribute to the development in several ways:

- Providing long views across the gardens, giving interest to those moving from one building to the next.
- Enabling residents to orientate themselves as the external spaces under the bridges each incorporate different features.
- Allowing views through the building, reducing its scale and the visual impact on the adjacent homes.

The internal layout is dementia friendly throughout, using visual cues to differentiate key areas and elements, helping residents and visitors to navigate independently and with confidence. All apartments are spacious; each has three habitable rooms, generous storage and private external amenity space, as recommended by the HAPPI Report.

The original cobbled courtyard, surrounded by the converted barns, has become a new 'village square'. Designed to host a range of social and wider community events, it links directly to the internal village street and public entrance. In contrast, the distinctive, new green spaces between the apartment blocks are sun-filled and sheltered – designed to encourage residents to take ownership and actively participate in outdoor activities.

The local authority undertook extensive public consultation involving local community groups. This was included in the PFI design brief to inform the design development throughout the competitive dialogue process. The Stoke County Council planning team were fully consulted at each design stage, and issued regular feedback to the design team to ensure that planning objectives and design quality were maintained throughout the process, resulting in an exemplar public–private sector development.

Through thoughtful orientation, a fabric-first approach and a well-researched materials specification, Willow Barns achieved a BREEAM rating of 'Excellent'. It was also awarded the Housing Design HAPPI Award for best completed project in 2017.

CASE STUDY 10

Fitch Court

DEVELOPMENT TYPE: Extra care housing

LOCATION: Somerleyton Road, Brixton Green, London

CLIENT: Igloo for Lambeth Council

ARCHITECT: Mæ

CONTRACTOR: Not known

CONSTRUCTION VALUE: £13.5m

COMPLETION DATE: Not known

NUMBER OF HOMES: 65 apartments (part of a wider masterplan for a total of 304 dwellings and 9,574 m² of non-residential uses)

TENURE MIX: 50% market rent, 10% affordable rent and 40% social rent

---

AVERAGE AGE OF RESIDENTS: 65+

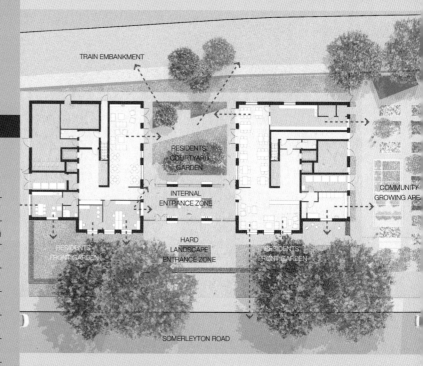

CONCEPT/RATIONALE

Set up in 2008, Brixton Green is an example of a community-led approach to regeneration. In November 2013, Lambeth Council agreed to develop the site in partnership with the community. A steering group was set up with representatives from the council, Brixton Green and the Ovalhouse Theatre. The ambition is for the whole mixed-use development (apart from the theatre) to be leased to a new community body for 250 years.

The site is long and narrow; an elevated railway viaduct runs along one side and an underground line crosses diagonally beneath. These constraints, along with the presence of a number of valuable, mature trees suggested a series of blocks with small footprints.

The design of the extra care block, Fitch Court, began with a careful arrangement of communal facilities and private spaces, based on the principles of progressive privacy. This allows residents to choose how and when they interact with their neighbours. The demands of the brief and the challenges posed by the site suggested a mid-rise solution with efficient lift and stair cores, adjacent to double-height winter gardens. Each of these year-round social spaces is shared by clusters of eight flats, promoting a level of resident ownership.

The apartments are spacious and flexible, arranged in two towers, each with four flats per floor, allowing everyone a dual aspect home. All look out onto either the street or the shared spaces ensuring a strong, visual connection with the wider neighbourhood.

←←← Ground floor plan.
←← Typical upper floor plan.
← Section through wintergarden.
↖ Street elevation.
↓ Section showing shared garden.

POINTS OF SPECIAL INTEREST

Any building that aspires to be 'fully future-proof' must consider sustainability in all its forms. By creating a building that will allow successive generations of older people to live independently for longer, the project is fulfilling a number of social and environmental objectives. By connecting to the Brixton Heat Network, Fitch Court should achieve a 35% reduction in carbon emissions, in line with London Plan targets. Passive energy measures and renewable initiatives such as a shared basement energy plant and rooftop PV panels will contribute further. The 'fabric-first' approach will limit heat loss through the facade and the scheme will have low energy lighting and mechanical ventilation with heat recovery throughout.

As older people are considered less as a separate group of vulnerable people that demand resources and funding, and more as a valued and vital expanding sector of society, it is important that housing standards for older people are adopted in mainstream provision. By collaborating on the wider masterplan, Mæ has enabled strategies for intergenerational inclusion to feed into the design of the new neighbourhood as a whole.

TESTIMONIAL

'The architects listened carefully and really took on board everybody's complaints, concerns and observations. They physically came and looked at some of our flats. People are very comfortable with what is on offer. This is not just building a block, it is building a community that feels family orientated. We'll be secure and sociable.'

CARLTON GUY,
TENANTS' REPRESENTATIVE AND FUTURE RESIDENT
OF FITCH COURT

CASE STUDY 11

Almshouse for the 21st Century

DEVELOPMENT TYPE: Contemporary urban almshouse

LOCATION: Bermondsey, London

CLIENT: United St Saviour Charity

ARCHITECT: Witherford Watson Mann Architects

CONTRACTOR: not appointed

CONSTRUCTION VALUE: undisclosed

COMPLETION DATE: anticipated 2020

NUMBER OF HOMES: 57 apartments (51 x 1 bed, 6 x 2 bed)

TENURE MIX: 100% social rent

AGE RANGE: 60+

> *... This seeks to break away from the tradition of providing a withdrawn and internally focused residents' lounge or meeting room. Instead, a publicly accessible shared cafe/lounge connects directly onto the high street.*

CONCEPT/RATIONALE

Over the coming years, the fastest growing age group in London will be the over-60s. Working closely with the United St Saviour Charity, the architects responded to this challenge by seeing it as an extremely positive one, requiring a different sort of imagination. Older people make a significant contribution to local places, local sociability, local perceptions of safety, local economies and the nurturing of young people – they are the critical part of the civil fabric of a 'good city'.

The design response is an 'Almshouse for the 21st century', an urban almshouse, located on an historic high street near to an important local centre in Bermondsey, south London. It specifically responds to the increasing problems of loneliness and its impacts on personal wellbeing and local health services. The individual homes are organised around a verdant, shared garden court – rich in textures and light, and embodying a strong sense of collective living. This seeks to break away from the tradition of providing a withdrawn and internally focused residents' lounge or meeting room. Instead, a publicly accessible shared cafe/lounge connects directly onto the high street – a generous sunlit room that reaches back into the garden court for non-residents to pop in for a coffee or to meet a friend.

← ← Ground floor plan.

← The building fronts onto the High Street.

↙ Generous, sociable walkways.

↓ The central garden court.

POINTS OF SPECIAL INTEREST

Lounge/cafe: In recognition that for many older people, sitting and watching the daily coming and going of life is stimulating and interesting , the shared cafe/lounge and a first-floor residents' gallery look directly onto the High Street. The architects observed that in almost every model of older people's housing they looked at these shared spaces were treated as some form of 'retreat' – highly privatised spaces buried within the interior of a scheme and facing onto private landscapes.

Responding to the fact that many older Londoners remain healthy and active much later in life and can make a critical contribution to local places and local social networks, the lounge/cafe has been arranged in a way that can accommodate small theatrical and musical performances from local groups and schools, operate as an occasional 'marketplace' for things made by residents, and a place to exchange knowledge between different generations.

Garden spaces: Within this extremely compact urban site, the almshouse is structured around a series of communal garden spaces, each with a distinctive character that supports diverse forms of social interaction. The atmosphere and design of each garden accommodates different activities. The southern wing steps down to two storeys to ensure that

the movement of the sun animates the central garden court, with its textured plants and water. The rear of the site is characterised by existing mature trees that create a shady woodland garden where a timber pavilion can be used for small group activities, yoga, reading and games. Between these two gardens, on the roof of the lower southern block, a residents' growing garden is created with raised beds, a greenhouse and external dining space.

Generous walkways: All residents will approach their homes along a generous glazed walkway that wraps around the garden court. Defining the interior of the court, the walkway will be full of light and shadows. Sliding timber and glass screens will make it possible to open up the facade, enabling the walkway to become a balcony onto the garden court that residents can occupy directly outside their own home. Residents will be encouraged to take ownership of these areas, with subtle demarcations in the tiled flooring indicating shared places for a couple of chairs or small table for plants. Each home will have a second aspect by borrowing daylight from the walkway into the kitchen and entrance hall. It is hoped that these generous walkways with their warm timber finishes and textures of the garden court will support sociability between residents.

CASE STUDY 12

Lodge Road

DEVELOPMENT TYPE: Independent living, residential care, respite and rehabilitation

LOCATION: Westminster, London

CLIENT: Central & Cecil Housing Trust

ARCHITECT: Ryder

CONTRACTOR: not appointed

CONSTRUCTION VALUE: undisclosed

COMPLETION DATE: not known (anticipated start date May 2018)

NUMBER OF HOMES: 159, comprising:
- 146 apartments (123 x 1 bed, 8 x 2 bed, 15 x fully accessible)
- 3 respite and rehabilitation suites
- 10 care units

TENURE MIX: 142 apartments for social rent and 17 at market rent

AVERAGE AGE OF RESIDENTS: 60–95 (based on the existing population)

> ❝ Co-design was at the heart of the process; the design team worked with the existing resident population to capture their aspirations from the outset.

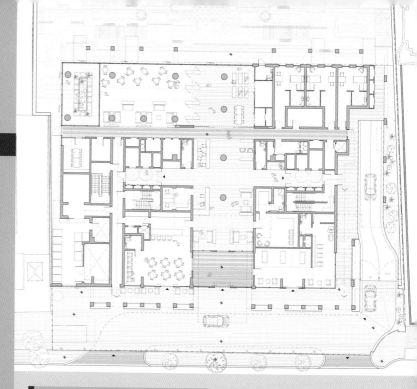

CONCEPT/RATIONALE

The Lodge Road development will replace the existing building on the site – Dora House, a 1960s block with its own distinctive character and community. The brief was clear: to reimagine the site to provide homes that would significantly improve the day-to-day lives of the residents; strengthening existing relationships and reinforcing ties with the surrounding community.

Co-design was at the heart of the process; the design team worked with the existing resident population to capture their aspirations from the outset. The process led to key design drivers, which were developed, tested and challenged.

The need to provide 'homes for life' that allowed residents to remain with their loved ones within the community they cherished, was paramount. This underpinned the core values of the client, Central & Cecil, to provide inspirational environments, establishing long-lasting communities where residents can remain in their home regardless of ability or need. Dora House previously offered predominantly small, inflexible bedsit accommodation, which was unable to meet residents' needs. Consequently, they had to leave when their support needs changed which in some instances meant to a care scheme outside of the Borough, breaking friendship groups.

←← Ground floor plan.

← Street view looking west.

↓ Frontage to Lodge Road.

→ Flexible 1 bed apartment (below) converts to two care rooms if required (above).

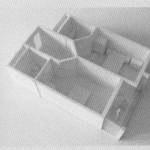

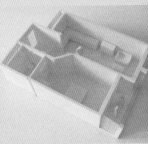

POINTS OF SPECIAL INTEREST

One of the key design elements is the creation of clustered living environments. Community is integral to the success of the development, with the client keen to strengthen the friendship groups that have developed in Dora House (some for over 50 years).

Although the development offers almost 160 apartments, the relatively small footprint and the clustering of apartments allows double-banked corridors to be avoided. There are two specific cluster types – independent living and care clusters.

- Independent living comprises groups of seven apartments located around a lift and circulation core. The majority of apartments have one bedroom but each cluster also includes a larger two bedroom or fully accessible apartment.

- The care clusters provide residents with an environment that offers greater levels of care as needed. These spaces are designed to provide ten en suite residential rooms, based around a central core. Operationally these are split into sub-clusters of five rooms, each with its own distinctive shared communal environment and carer. Overnight the sub-clusters are combined allowing one carer to oversee ten residents.

Central & Cecil will provide 24-hour care to residents, allowing them to remain within the development and continue to make full use of the shared facilities. This will greatly benefit existing community links and could, for example, allow a couple in which one partner is living with dementia to be cared for in the care cluster, while their partner remains within the independent living cluster.

Flexibility is vital to Central & Cecil's approach, with the cluster arrangements allowing the building to adapt in the future if necessary to cater for changing demographics and / or an evolving business plan. The one-bedroom apartments are designed to allow for easy conversion to two care rooms, to further increase the flexibility. An important component of the project brief was to encourage community, enable new relationships to form and strengthen existing links. Key to this was ensuring that residents could remain in the building regardless of changing needs.

CASE STUDY 13

Ørestad Retirement Home

DEVELOPMENT TYPE: Retirement home, municipal extra care/care home

LOCATION: Ørestad Syd, Copenhagen

CLIENT: KAB (housing association) for the municipality

ARCHITECT: JJW Arkitekter

CONTRACTOR: NCC

CONSTRUCTION VALUE: 185m Danish kroner

COMPLETION DATE: 2012

NUMBER OF HOMES/APARTMENTS: 114

TENURE MIX: rent, subsided by the municipality

AVERAGE AGE OF RESIDENTS: 84

█ CONCEPT/RATIONALE

Designed by local architects, JJW Arkitekter, and built in 2011–12, this development is located in Ørestad, one of three new mixed-use residential areas being created to cater for Copenhagen's rapidly expanding population. Referred to as a retirement home, an equivalent facility in England would fall somewhere between extra care and a residential care home. As is typical in Demark, it was commissioned and funded by the municipality; in this case, in conjunction with a housing association, KAB, who now manages it.

In order to qualify for a place, it is necessary to obtain certification from a doctor that the applicant is no longer able to live independently without considerable help. Rising demand means that places are being allocated to people with higher care needs than was previously the case, and a large proportion of the Ørestad residents are living with dementia. Living and care costs are subsided by the municipality, but the amount is determined by means testing; while some residents pay nothing, others pay a substantial proportion.

Even in a modern, mixed-use neighbourhood, this exuberant building, which wraps around two prominent street corners, stands out. While it observes the strict, local design codes, the external massing is broken down into vertical sections – each painted a different shade of green or yellow. The strong colours and generous 'boxed balconies', offset and sliced-off at jaunty angles, differentiate it from its more sombre neighbours. The balconies give human scale and provide shelter in this windy, low-lying neighbourhood.

←← The main facade with its playful but practical balconies.

← The semi-public courtyard.

↙ Stylish sitting space.

↓ Shared dining area.

POINTS OF SPECIAL INTEREST

JJW Arkitekter attaches a great deal of importance to the briefing and early design stages, which they see as collaborative and iterative processes. The primary goals are simple – equity, wellbeing and homeliness. The aim is to support independent living for as long as possible within a safe, healthy and non-clinical environment.

Rather than a concierge-style reception desk, the generous 5 metre high ground-floor entrance area opens to a kitchen counter surrounded by bookshelves, part of a flexible social area used for eating as well as classes and gatherings. This space, and other facilities, including a hairdressing salon and dental surgery, is open to the community.

Danish regulations require a minimum of 65m² internal floor space per person, which can be achieved by a combination of private and shared space. At Ørestad, the private apartments are arranged in household groups of 10–12, arranged around a bright shared living/eating/cooking space with access to the balcony. With an internal floor area of approximately 38m², the compact, two-room apartments are light, airy and flexible. A large, glazed, sliding door allows the living space (which includes a small kitchen area for making drinks and snacks) to be opened up to the large, single bedroom with en suite shower. The two rooms are a similar size and some less mobile residents have chosen to make the room with the balcony their bedroom. The design facilitates personalisation – from letterboxes to private entrances and interiors, enriching the living environment as a result.

Meals are prepared in the group kitchens which adjoin the relaxed but stylish, shared dining spaces. Residents generally choose to eat together and are encouraged to help with food preparation and laying the table. Despite the contemporary setting, classic Danish furniture from the 1940–60s evokes eras familiar to those who live there. Strong colours stand out against a mainly white backdrop and contribute to identity and wayfinding. Materials generally are natural, tactile and durable.

JJW strongly believes that buildings must work as well for staff as they do for residents. Administrative areas are ergonomically designed and staff rest rooms are quiet and spacious. The three-sided building encloses a sheltered, planted courtyard which is accessible from the adjoining streets, as well as from the building itself; a sunny, restful semi-private place for residents, staff and anyone else who wishes to use it.

NOTE

Text written by Julia Park following a visit to the building and an interview with Ole Hornbek, Architect and Creative Director, and Pawel Antoni Lange, Head of Communications and PR, at JJW Arkitekter.

CASE STUDY 14

Meadow View

DEVELOPMENT TYPE: Specialist residential care facility and community care centre

LOCATION: Darley Dale, Derbyshire

CLIENT: Derbyshire County Council

ARCHITECT: Glancy Nicholls Architects

CONTRACTOR: Balfour Beatty

CONSTRUCTION VALUE: £9m

COMPLETION DATE: January 2016

NUMBER OF ROOM: 32 (16 long-term and 16 short-term bedroom suites)

AGE RANGE: Not known

CONCEPT/RATIONALE

Sitting on a sloping site within an area of outstanding natural beauty within the Darley Dales, the contemporary design of this bespoke care facility responds to the sloping site and elements of the local vernacular, while maximising spectacular views of the open countryside.

The building, which is adjacent to an existing hospital, is specially designed to accommodate the particular needs of older residents with severe dementia, and is the focal point for delivering services to older people with this and other complex needs. It promotes an individual approach to independence, wellbeing and dignity, and it was imperative that it did not appear institutional.

In addition to the 32 en suite bedrooms, the building provides a restaurant/cafe, hairdresser, activity rooms, a full production kitchen, consultancy rooms and treatment areas. These facilities invite the general public to be involved with the centre, allowing residents to remain independent and socially integrated while being cared for. Meadow View also provides intermediate care to help people return home after being in hospital, accommodates day and respite services to help people stay at home, and provides a focal point for carers. It offers advice, practical support and access to other organisations and services, including:

- Derbyshire County Council Information Portal
- Alzheimer's Society
- Age Concern Derbyshire

- Derbyshire Library Service
- Bookings for professional social care
- Referrals via Call Derbyshire.

← Ground floor plan.
→ Site Plan.
→→ Top-lit, dry-stone, spine wall.
↓ Front elevation to Bakewell Road.

POINTS OF SPECIAL INTEREST

The spatial relationship of the different functions of the building resulted in the accommodation being split over three main blocks. Working with the topography, these blocks sit across the site on three plateaus, allowing the scheme to be integral within the natural landscape.

The central block incudes the main entrance, which in turn leads to the reception area, general waiting and communal facilities. This allows the public to use the new services without having to access the two residential blocks; the long-term accommodation on one side, and the short-term on the other.

The building is designed to be fully accessible and easy to use – responding to the need to minimise anxiety and confusion. Activity spaces, located at the ends of the corridors within the bedroom blocks, encourage residents to gather informally, as well as offering views and access into and out of the building.

The use of locally sourced natural Derbyshire stone was key to the contemporary design. The main, linear dry-stone wall acts as a unifying spine, helping to bind the various spaces of the building together. This contrasts sharply with the ashlar stone cladding, which provides crisp edges to the building, framing the elevations.

All materials were sustainably sourced, reducing the carbon footprint, which in turn reduced the overall cost of the project and enhanced the BREEAM score. A wild-flower meadow roof gives the building a living element that changes with the local ecosystem throughout the seasons, and provides high levels of insulation.

The enlightened client played an active role throughout the design process, and recognised the long-term value of investing in high-quality buildings and spaces, using robust, low-maintenance materials. The building has been designed with ease of care in mind, which will result in staffing efficiencies and lower costs. Through careful design and specification, Meadow View has exceeded expectations while remaining within budget.

CASE STUDY 15

De Hogeweyk

DEVELOPMENT TYPE: Dementia care village

LOCATION: Weesp, Holland

CLIENT: Vivium Zorggroep, Huizen (a private foundation, mostly government funded by the Dutch National Health system)

ARCHITECT: Molenaar & Bol & VanDillen Architecten

CONTRACTOR: Heijmerink Bouw B.V.

CONSTRUCTION VALUE: €19.3 million

COMPLETION DATE: December 2009

NUMBER OF HOMES: A total of 150 residents accommodated in 23 apartments (households)

AGE RANGE: 60–105

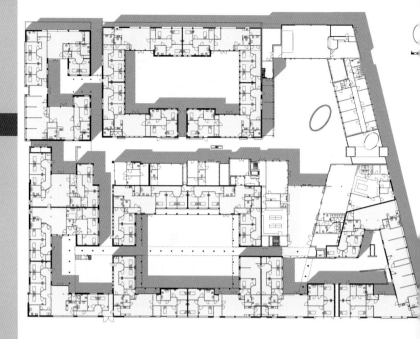

▎ CONCEPT/RATIONALE

In 1992, the management team of 'Hogewey', a traditional nursing home in Weesp in Holland, decided to do things differently. The team sat down to decide what should be done to develop a form of care for people living with serious, advanced dementia. They felt a strong commitment to develop a form of care that would be acceptable to, and for, their own families, parents, friends – and their 'future selves' – a normal life for people living with severe dementia.

The resulting 'Hogeweyk Care Concept' represents a cultural shift in care for the elderly, a deviation from a medical system to a social, relational system. The focus is on remaining healthy and continuing to enjoy a normal and sociable life, despite dementia and other health problems that may occur.

The development team, Vivium Zorggroep, and the architects, Molenaar & Bol & VanDillen Architecten, have created a purpose-built, self-contained village named De Hogeweyk. Unassuming, low-rise brick buildings flank a boulevard and a variety of public spaces and gardens, including a town square with a fountain. There is a supermarket, cafe/restaurant and theatre, and though the village is gated to keep residents safe, some facilities are open to the public.

Carers make up the majority of the 250 staff, but home companions, club leaders, maintenance personnel and practitioners are among the rest. The staff wear ordinary clothes (not uniforms) and aim to make life as normal as possible for the residents.

←← Ground floor plan.

← Public square with fountains.

↙ Street view of the residential blocks.

→ Sheltered outdoor sitting area.

POINTS OF SPECIAL INTEREST

Each of the 23 apartments, or 'households', is home to six or seven residents. The internal designs are based on four themed lifestyles to allow residents to be housed in an environment that they will find comfortable and familiar.

• *'Stads'*: urban, for those who are used to living in a town or city
• *'Huiselijk Traditioneel'*: traditional, for homemakers
• *'Formeel'*: formal, with an aristocratic Dutch feel
• *'Cultureel'*: cosmopolitan, for those brought up with theatre and cinema.

These four typologies offer different interior characters, play different types of music and offer different types of food, cooked and served in different ways. Each resident has a large bedroom and shares a living room and a kitchen/dining room with other household members, taking part in cooking and other activities as they wish.

All staff are trained professionals. Every employee and volunteer also receives training in hospitality, dementia, the 'Hogeweyk Care Concept' and the various lifestyles. Every household has a dedicated team of well-trained staff who know the group of residents very well. They understand what is important to each of them and are familiar with the lifestyle and

daily routines that are specific to each house. The team members will support (but not take over) each person in a way that allows him, or her, to manage and enjoy their life in their own individual way, day by day.

People in Holland are free to choose the nursing home they wish. The €6000 monthly cost per person for De Hogeweyk is met by the Dutch national health system, and is equivalent to the cost of living in a traditional Dutch care home. The budget given by the state is effectively all-inclusive and covers accommodation, facilities, food and drink, staff costs, medication etc. Carers report that residents require less medication than they needed in the former care home, enjoy a better quality of life and have a more positive frame of mind.

Endnotes

EPIGRAPH

1   World Health Organization, 'Global age-friendly cities project', 2018, http://www.who.int/ageing/projects/age_friendly_cities/en/ (accessed 8 February, 2018).

PREFACE

2   Matthew Barac and Julia Park, *Housing Our Ageing Population: Panel for Innovation (HAPPI1)*, Homes and Communities Agency, 2009, https://www.gov.uk/government/uploads/system/uploads/attachament_data/file/378171/happi_final_report_-_031209.pdf (accessed 8 February, 2018).

3   Foresight, *Future of an Ageing Population*, Government Office for Science, 2016, https://www.gov.uk/government/uploads/system/uploads/attachment_data/file/535187/gs-16-10-future-of-an-ageing-population.pdf (accessed 8 February, 2018).

4   Ian Copeman and Jeremy Porteus, *Housing Our Ageing Population: Learning from councils meeting the needs of our ageing population*, Local Government Association, 2017, https://www.local.gov.uk/sites/default/files/documents/5.17%20-%20Housing%20our%20ageing%20population_07_0.pdf (accessed 8 February 2018).

CHAPTER 1.0

5   Ludi Simpson and Anne Berrington, 'Explaining changes in household size', Powerpoint presentation, (nd), http://www.lse.ac.uk/socialPolicy/Researchcentresandgroups/BSPS/dayMeetings/Explaining-changes-in-family-size.pdf (accessed 8 February 2018).

6   The King's Fund, 'Demography: Future trends', part of the Time to Think Differently programme, 2018, https://www.kingsfund.org.uk/time-to-think-differently/trends/demography/life-expectancy_ (accessed 8 February 2018).

7   Age UK, *Older People as Volunteers Evidence Review*, 2011, http://www.ageuk.org.uk/Documents/EN-GB/For-professionals/Research/OlderPeopleAsVolunteers.pdf?dtrk=true (accessed 8 February 2018).

8   The Adaptation and Resilience in the Context of Change (ARCC) network, 'Are you interested in improved health and wellbeing for our ageing society?', (nd), http://www.arcc-network.org.uk/health-wellbeing/ageing-mobility/ (accessed 8 February 2018).

9   Foresight, *Future of an Ageing Population*. (Original data source: Dominic Abrams, Christin-Melanie Vauclair and Hannah Swift, *Predictors of Attitudes to Age Across Europe*, Department of Work and Pensions Research Report No. 735, 2011, https://www.gov.uk/government/uploads/system/uploads/attachment_data/file/214509/rrep735.pdf (accessed 8 February 2018).

10 Quoted in Sophie Handler, *An Alternative Age-Friendly Handbook*, RIBA/UK Urban Ageing Consortium/MICRA/Age UK, 2016, https://www.architecture.com/knowledge-and-resources/resources-landing-page/age-friendly-handbook (accessed 8 February 2018).

11 David Drew, 'Sheltered housing', Hansard HC Deb, col 265WH, 14 June 2000, https://publications.parliament.uk/pa/cm199900/cmhansrd/vo000614/halltext/00614h05.htm (accessed 8 February 2018).

12 Anne-Marie Nicholson, *Homes for the Third Age: A design guide for extra care sheltered housing*, Housing Corporation and Hanover Housing Group, 1997.

13 Text adapted from 'A brief history of housing for older people', RM architects, 2015, http://rm-architects. com/ideas/2015/6/26/a-brief-history-of-housing-for-older-people (accessed 8 February 2018).

14 Richard Best and Jeremy Porteus, *Housing Our Ageing Population: Plan for implementation* (*HAPPI 2*), APPG inquiry report, Housing LIN, 2012, https:// www.housinglin.org.uk/_assets/Resources/Housing/ Support_materials/Other_reports_and_guidance/ Housing_our_Ageing_Population_Plan_for_ Implementation.pdf (accessed 8 February 2018).

15 Barac and Park, *Housing Our Ageing Population*.

16 Barac and Park, *Housing Our Ageing Population*.

17 Housing Design Awards website, http://hdawards. org// (accessed 8 February 2018).

18 David Sinclair and Helen Creighton, *Opportunity Knocks: Designing solutions for an ageing society* International Longevity Centre, 2015, http://www. ilcuk.org.uk/index.php/publications/publication_ details/opportunity_knocks_designing_solutions_ for_an_ageing_society (accessed 8 February 2018).

19 Lifetime Homes website, www.lifetimehomes.org.uk (accessed 8 February 2018).

20 HM Government, *Approved Document M – Access to and Use of Buildings: Volume 1 – Dwellings (2015 edition incorporating 2016 amendments)*, 2016, https://www. gov.uk/government/publications/access-to-and-use-of-buildings-approved-document-m (accessed 8 February 2018).

21 DCLG with DoH and DWP, *Lifetime Neighbourhoods*, DCLG, December 2011, http://www.cpa.org.uk/cpa/ lifetimehomes.pdf (accessed 8 February 2018).

22 Ed Harding, *Towards Lifetime Neighbourhoods: Designing sustainable communities for all.* International Longevity Centre UK and DCLG, November 2007,

http://www.ilc-alliance.org/images/uploads/ publication-pdfs/pdf_pdf_40.pdf (accessed 8 February 2018).

23 Claudia Wood, *The Top of the Ladder*, Demos, 2013, https://www.demos.co.uk/files/TopoftheLadder-web. pdf?1378922386 (accessed 8 February 2018).

24 HM Government, *Laying the Foundations: A housing strategy for England*, DCLG, November 2011, https:// www.gov.uk/government/publications/laying-the-foundations-a-housing-strategy-for-england--2 (accessed 8 February 2018).

25 Ministry of Housing, Communities and Local Government and the Rt Hon Grant Shapps, 'New deal will help older people live at home for longer', 3 January 2012, https://www.gov.uk/government/ news/new-deal-will-help-older-people-live-at-home-for-longer (accessed 8 February 2018).

26 Department for Communities and Local Government, *National Planning Policy Framework*, DCLG, March 2012, https://www.gov.uk/government/uploads/ system/uploads/attachment_data/file/6077/2116950. pdf (accessed 8 February 2018).

27 Ministry of Housing, Communities and Local Government, 'Planning practice guidance', 29 November 2016, last updated 28 July 2017, https:// www.gov.uk/government/collections/planning-practice-guidance (accessed 8 February 2018).

28 Ministry of Housing, Communities and Local Government and the Rt Hon Brandon Lewis MP, 'Planning update March 2015', Written statement to Parliament, 25 March 2015, https://www.gov.uk/ government/news/better-homes-and-bungalows-for-britains-older-people (accessed 8 February 2018).

29 Department for Communities and Local Government, 'Fixing our broken housing market', February 2017, https://www.gov.uk/government/uploads/system/ uploads/attachment_data/file/590464/Fixing_our_ broken_housing_market_-_print_ready_version.pdf (accessed 8 February 2018).

CHAPTER 2.0

30   Claudia Wood, *The Affordability of Retirement Housing*, APPG inquiry report, Housing LIN, 2014, https://www.housinglin.org.uk/_assets/Resources/Housing/OtherOrganisation/Demos_APPG_REPORT.pdf (accessed 10 February 2018).

31   Sam Clark, *Retirement Living Explained: A guide for planning and design professionals*, Churchill Retirement Housing, 2017, https://www.churchillretirement.co.uk/assets/Retirement-Living-Explained-Planning-Report-web.pdf (accessed 10 February 2018).

32   Moyra Riseborough, Peter Fletcher and Denise Gillie, *Extra Care Housing – What is it in 2015?*, Factsheet 1, Housing LIN, 2015, http://www.housinglin.org.uk/_assets/Resources/Housing/Housing_advice/Extra_Care_Housing_-_What_is_it_2015.pdf (accessed 10 February 2018).

33   Royal Institute of British Architects, *Housing Matters: Twenty ways to solve the housing crisis*, RIBA, 2017, https://www.architecture.com/knowledge-and-resources/resources-landing-page/housing-matters (accessed 10 February 2018).

34   Clark, *Retirement Living Explained*.

35   Lisa Birchall, 'BME Elders Housing and Health Promotion Project', Case Study 131, Housing LIN, 2017, http://www.housinglin.org.uk/_library/Resources/Housing/Practice_examples/Housing_LIN_case_studies/HLIN_CaseStudy_131_BMEElders.pdf (accessed 10 February 2018).

36   PegasusLife website, https://www.pegasuslife.co.uk/about-us/crafting-an-experience/ (accessed 10 February 2018).

37   Richard Best and Jeremy Porteus, *Housing Our Ageing Population: Positive ideas (HAPPI 3)*, APPG inquiry report, Housing LIN, 2017, https://www.housinglin.org.uk/_assets/Resources/Housing/Support_materials/Other_reports_and_guidance/HAPPI3_Report_2016.pdf (accessed 10 February 2018).

38   Stonewall Housing, *Building Safe Choices: LGBT housing futures: a feasibility study*, June 2016, http://www.buildingsafechoices.org.uk/wp-content/uploads/2016/06/BuildingSafeChoices_full.pdf, 2016 (accessed 10 February 2018).

39   Whiteley Village website, http://whiteleyvillage.org.uk/about-us/ (accessed 10 February 2018).

40   Les Mayhew, Ben Rickayzen and David Smith, *Does Living in a Retirement Village Extend Life Expectancy? The case of Whiteley Village*, International Longevity Centre UK and Cass Business School, 2017, http://www.ilcuk.org.uk/images/uploads/publication-pdfs/ILC-UK_-_Does_Living_in_a_Retirement_Village_Extend_Life_Expectancy_-_Web_version_updated.pdf (accessed 10 February 2018).

41   Carol Holland, Danielle Clarkesmith, Jill Collins, Barbara Hagger, Amanda Kay, Jess Lambie, Leanne Liddell and Stuart Wallis, 'Collaborative research between Aston Research Centre for Healthy Ageing (ARCHA) and the ExtraCare Charitable Trust', Aston University, 2015, http://www.aston.ac.uk/EasySiteWeb/GatewayLink.aspx?alId=245545 (accessed 10 February 2018).

42   Department of Health, *Care Homes for Older People: National Minimum Standards, Care Homes Regulations* (3rd edn), Department of Health, 2003, http://www.dignityincare.org.uk/_library/resources/dignity/csipcomment/csci_national_minimum_standards.pdf (accessed 10 February 2018).

43   Stephen Cousins, 'New tool to improve dementia design', *RIBA Journal*, 20 March 2017, https://www.ribaj.com/products/living-with-dementia (accessed 8 February 2018).

44   Alzheimer's Society, *Dementia-Friendly Housing Charter: Guidance on delivering a dementia-friendly approach to housing*, March 2017, https://www.alzheimers.org.uk/download/downloads/id/3485/dementia-friendly_housing_charter.pdf (accessed 10 February 2018).

45 Department of Health, *Health Building Note 08-02. Dementia-Friendly Health and Social Care Environments*, March 2015, https://www.gov.uk/government/publications/dementia-friendly-health-and-social-care-environments-hbn-08-02 (accessed 10 February 2018).

46 Jim Dunton, 'Sheffield firm designs home for Alzheimer's sufferer', *Building Design*, 5 January 2017, http://www.bdonline.co.uk/news/sheffield-firm-designs-home-for-alzheimer's-sufferer/5085574.article (accessed 10 February 2018).

47 University of Stirling Dementia Services Development Centre website, http://dementia.stir.ac.uk/information/dementia-research (accessed 10 February 2018).

48 Dia Soilemezi, 'Living well with dementia at home', *RIBA Journal*, 29 November 2016, https://www.ribaj.com/intelligence/living-well-with-dementia-at-home (accessed 10 February 2018).

49 Women's Royal Voluntary Service (WRVS), *Gold Age Pensioners: Valuing the socio-economic contribution of older people in the UK*, March 2011, https://www.royalvoluntaryservice.org.uk/Uploads/Documents/gold_age_report_2011.pdf (accessed 10 February 2018).

50 Ibid.

51 Carey Reed, 'Dutch nursing home offers rent-free housing to students', *PBS Newshour*, 5 April 2015, http://www.pbs.org/newshour/rundown/dutch-retirement-home-offers-rent-free-housing-students-one-condition/ (accessed 10 February 2018).

52 Kirstie Brewer, 'Why young people are renting rooms in a Helsinki care home', *The Guardian*, 21 June 2017, https://www.theguardian.com/society/2017/jun/21/young-people-renting-rooms-helsinki-care-home (accessed 10 February 2018).

53 *RIBA Journal*, 'MultiGen Awards: Solving a problem of our time', October 2017, https://www.ribaj.com/products/solving-a-problem-of-our-times-norbord-multi-gen-awards (accessed 10 February 2018).

54 Cassie Barton, *Home Ownership and Renting: Demographics*, House of Commons Library Briefing Paper CBP 7706,9 June 2017, http://researchbriefings.files.parliament.uk/documents/CBP-7706/CBP-7706.pdf (accessed 10 February 2018).

55 NHS England, 'Healthy New Towns' project, (nd), https://www.england.nhs.uk/ourwork/innovation/healthy-new-towns/ (accessed 10 February 2018).

56 WRVS, *Gold Age Pensioners*.

57 Best and Porteus, *Housing Our Ageing Population (HAPPI 3)*.

58 Adam Park, Friederike Ziegler and Sarah Wigglesworth, *Designing with Downsizers: The next generation of 'downsizer homes' for an active third age (DWELL)*, University of Sheffield / Housing LIN, 2016, https://www.housinglin.org.uk/_assets/DWELL_DesigningWithDownsizers.pdf (accessed 10 February 2018).

59 University of York, 'Buildings in the making: A sociological exploration of architecture in the context of health and social care', August 2015–July 2018, https://www.york.ac.uk/sociology/research/current-research/nettleton,-daryl-martin-chrissy-buse/#tab-1 (accessed 10 February 2018).

CHAPTER 3.0

60 National Fire Chiefs Council, *Fire Safety in Specialised Housing*, NFCC, 2017, https://www.nationalfirechiefs.org.uk/write/MediaUploads/NFCC%20Guidance%20publications/NFCC_Specialised_Housing_Guidance_-_Copy.pdf (accessed 12 February 2018).

61 Manchester City of Trees website, 'Why trees: Health and wellbeing', http://www.cityoftrees.org.uk/why-trees-health-wellbeing (accessed 12 February 2018).

62 Equal Arts website, 'Henpower', https://www.equalarts.org.uk/our-work/henpower (accessed 12 February 2018).

CHAPTER 4.0

63 The Royal Society for the Prevention of Accidents, 'Older people safety', 2016, https://www.rospa.com/home-safety/advice/older-people/ (accessed 12 February 2018).

64 Office of the Deputy Prime Minister, *A Sure Start to Later Life: Ending inequalities for older people*, ODPM, January 2006, http://www.cpa.org.uk/cpa/seu_final_report.pdf, 2006 (accessed 12 February 2018).

65 Wood, *Top of the Ladder*.

66 Ibid., and Park et al, *Designing with Downsizers*.

67 Motion Spot website, www.motionspot.co.uk (accessed 12 February 2018).

68 Rajat Gupta, Gordon Walker, Alan Lewis, Laura Barnfield, Matt Gregg and Louis Neven, 'Care provision fit for a future climate', Joseph Rowntree Foundation, 2016, https://www.jrf.org.uk/report/care-provision-fit-future-climate (accessed 12 February 2018).

69 Lifetime Homes website, www.lifetimehomes.org.uk (accessed 8 February 2018).

70 Habinteg, *Wheelchair Housing Design Guide* (3rd edn), RIBA Publishing, 2018.

71 Department for Communities and Local Government, *Technical Housing Standards: Nationally described space standard*, March 2015, https://www.gov.uk/government/uploads/system/uploads/attachment_data/file/524531/160519_Nationally_Described_Space_Standard____Final_Web_version.pdf (accessed 12 February 2018).

CHAPTER 5.0

72 Newcastle City Futures, 'Future Homes: Future housing for an ageing society' project website, http://www.newcastlecityfutures.org/projects/future-homes/ (accessed 13 February 2018).

73 A Tamagotchi is a small handheld 'digital pet'. The player has to raise the pet as it grows during the game by feeding it virtual food, keeping it clean so it doesn't get ill and protecting it from predators.

74 Design Council, 'Living well with dementia' web resource, http://www.designcouncil.org.uk/resources/case-study/living-well-dementia (accessed 13 February 2018).

75 Foresight, *Future of an Ageing Population*.

76 Ibid.

77 ARCC network, 'Are you interested in improved health and wellbeing?'

78 Park et al., *Designing with Downsizers*.

79 Ibid.

80 Bill Davies, *For Future Living: Innovative approaches to joining up housing and health*, IPPR North, 2014, http://ippr.org/read/for-future-living-innovative-approaches-to-joining-up-housing-and-health# (accessed 13 February 2018).

81 Harding, *Towards Lifetime Neighbourhoods*.

82 NHS Information Centre, Adult Social Care Team, *'Registered blind and partially sighted people year ending 31 March 2011 England'*, NHS Information Centre, 1 September 2011, http://content.digital.nhs.uk/catalogue/PUB01687/peop-regi-blin-part-sigh-eng-11-rep.pdf (accessed 13 February 2018).

83 Margaret Martin, *Falls in Older People with Sight Loss: A review of emerging research and key action points,* Research Discussion Paper No 12, Thomas Pocklington Trust, June 2013.

http://pocklington-trust.org.uk/wp-content/
uploads/2013/06/Falls-in-Older-People-with-Sight-
Loss.pdf (accessed 14 February 2018).

84   Hawkins Brown, *What Clients Think of Architects:
Feedback from the 'working with architects' client survey
2016*, Royal Institute of British Architects, November
2016, https://www.hawkinsbrown.com/research/
speaking-out/what-do-clients-think-of-architects
(accessed 14 February 2018).

85   RIBA and Rowena Hay, Simon Bradbury, Dylan
Dixon, Kat Martindale, Flora Samuel and Alex Tait,
*Building Knowledge: Pathways to post occupancy
evaluation,* Value of Architects, University of
Reading, AHRC and RIBA, 2016, https://www.
architecture.com/-/media/gathercontent/post-
occupancy-evaluation/additional-documents/
buildingknowledgepathwaystopoepdf.pdf (accessed
14 February 2018).

86   Elderly Accommodation Counsel website, www.eac.
org.uk (accessed 14 February 2018).

87   University of Sheffield, *EVOLVE Tool – Evaluation of
older people's living environments*, Housing LIN, https://
www.housinglin.org.uk/_assets/Resources/Housing/
Support_materials/Other_reports_and_guidance/
evolve_toolkit.zip, 2010 (accessed 14 February 2018).

88   The King's Fund, 'Environments of care for people
with dementia' web resource, https://www.
kingsfund.org.uk/projects/enhancing-healing-
environment/ehe-in-dementia-care (accessed 14
February 2018).

89   Sinclair and Creighton, *Opportunity Knocks.*

90   Ibid.

91   Ibid.

92   Ibid.

CHAPTER 6.0

93   Comptroller and Auditor General, *Discharging
Older Patients From Hospital*, Session 2016–17, HC
18, National Audit Office, https://www.nao.org.uk/
wp-content/uploads/2015/12/Discharging-older-
patients-from-hospital.pdf (accessed 15 February
2018).

Further reading

Two key websites contain comprehensive design-related resources relating to age-friendly and accessible housing:

https://www.zotero.org/groups/234052/riba_research/items/collectionKey/ITFIKCH2

https://www.housinglin.org.uk/Topics/browse/Design-building/

To accompany this publication, the authors have also produced a more comprehensive reading list which is available at: https://www.housinglin.org.uk/RIBA-age-friendly-housing/

See also: http://www.levittbernstein.co.uk/research-writing/age-friendly-housing/

Select bibliography

The Adaptation and Resilience in the Context of Change (ARCC) network, 'Are you interested in improved health and wellbeing for our ageing society?' (nd), http://www.arcc-network.org.uk/health-wellbeing/ageing-mobility/ (accessed 8 February 2018).

Matthew Barac and Julia Park, J. *Housing Our Ageing Population: Panel for innovation*, Homes and Communities Agency, 2009, https://www.gov.uk/government/uploads/system/uploads/attachment_data/file/378171/happi_final_report_-_031209.pdf (accessed 15 February 2018).

Richard Best and Jeremy Porteus, *Housing Our Ageing Population: Positive ideas (HAPPI 3)*, APPG inquiry report, Housing LIN, 2017, https://www.housinglin.org.uk/_assets/Resources/Housing/Support_materials/Other_reports_and_guidance/HAPPI3_Report_2016.pdf (accessed 10 February 2018).

Sam Clark. *Retirement Living Explained: A guide for planning and design professionals*, Churchill Retirement Living, 2017, https://www.churchillretirement.co.uk/assets/Retirement-Living-Explained-Planning-Report-web.pdf (accessed 15 February 2018).

Ian Copeman and Jeremy Porteus. J. *Housing Our Ageing Population: Learning from councils meeting the needs of our ageing population*, Local Government Association, 2017, https://www.local.gov.uk/sites/default/files/documents/5.17%20-%20Housing%20our%20ageing%20population_07_0.pdf (accessed 15 February 2017).

Foresight, *Future of an Ageing Population*, Government Office for Science, 2016, https://www.gov.uk/government/uploads/system/uploads/attachment_data/file/535187/gs-16-10-future-of-an-ageing-population.pdf (accessed 15 February 2018).

Habinteg, *Wheelchair Housing Design Guide* (3rd edn), RIBA Publishing, 2018.

Bill Halsall and Dr Rob MacDonald. R. *Design for Dementia: Volume 1 – A Guide*, The Halsall Lloyd Partnership, 2015, http://www.hlpdesign.com/images/case_studies/Vol1.pdf (accessed 14 February 2018).

Bill Halsall and Dr Rob MacDonald. R. *Design for Dementia: Volume 2 – Research Projects*, The Halsall Lloyd Partnership, 2015, http://www.hlpdesign.com/images/case_studies/Vol2.pdf (accessed 14 February 2018).

Sophie Handler. *An Alternative Age-Friendly Handbook*, RIBA/UK Urban Ageing Consortium/MICRA/Age UK, 2016, https://www.architecture.com/knowledge-and-resources/resources-landing-page/age-friendly-handbook (accessed 15 February 2018).

Ed Harding. *Towards Lifetime Neighbourhoods: Designing sustainable communities for all.* International Longevity Centre UK and Department for Communities and Local Government, November 2007, http://www.ilc-alliance.org/images/uploads/publication-pdfs/pdf_pdf_40.pdf (accessed 8 February 2018).

Homes and Communities Agency, *Non-Mainstream Housing Design Guidance: Literature review*, HCA, 2012, http://webarchive.nationalarchives.gov.uk/20140805123756/https://www.homesandcommunities.co.uk/download-doc/6434/10967 (accessed 15 February 2018).

House of Commons, Communities and Local Government Committee, *Housing for Older People*, Second Report of Session 2017–19, HC 370, 5 February 2018, https://publications.parliament.uk/pa/cm201719/cmselect/cmcomloc/370/370.pdf (accessed 9 February 2018).

Legal and General Group, *Last Time Buyers*, Legal & General/CEBR, December 2015, https://www.legalandgeneralgroup.com/assets/portal/files/pdf_175.pdf (accessed 15 February 2018).

Lloyd, J. *Valuing Retirement Housing: Exploring the economic effects of specialist housing for older people*, Strategic Society Centre, August 2016, http://strategicsociety.org.uk/wp-content/uploads/2016/08/Valuing-Retirement-Housing.pdf (accessed 15 February 2018).

National House Building Council Foundation, *The Connected Home: Designing and building technology into today's new homes*, NHBC Foundation, 2016, https://www.nhbcfoundation.org/publication/the-connected-home/ (accessed 15 February 2018).

National House Building Council Foundation, *Moving Insights from the Over-55s: What homes do they buy?*, NHBC Foundation, 2017, https://www.nhbcfoundation.org/publication/moving-insights-from-the-over-55s-what-homes-do-they-buy/ (accessed 15 February 2018).

Adam Park, Friederike Ziegler and Sarah Wigglesworth, *Designing with Downsizers: The next generation of 'downsizer homes' for an active third age (DWELL)*, 2016, University of Sheffield / Housing LIN, https://www.housinglin.org.uk/_assets/DWELL_DesigningWithDownsizers.pdf (accessed 15 February 2018).

James Parkinson, Will Hunter, Matthew Barac, *Silver Linings: The active third age and the city*, RIBA, 2013, http://www.buildingfutures.org.uk/assets/downloads/MID_RIBA_Silver_linings_161013_v2.pdf (accessed 4 July 2017).

Royal Town Planning Institute, *Dementia and Town Planning: Creating better environments for people living with dementia*, RTPI, 2017, http://www.rtpi.org.uk/media/2213533/dementia_and_town_planning_final.compressed.pdf (accessed 16 February 2018).

David Sinclair and Helen Creighton. *Opportunity Knocks: Designing solutions for an ageing society*, International Longevity Centre UK, 2015, http://www.ilcuk.org.uk/index.php/publications/publication_details/opportunity_knocks_designing_solutions_for_an_ageing_society (accessed 16 February 2018).

Sonia Sodha. Silver Chic: *The future of retirement housing and care,* Anchor Trust, 2015, http://www.anchor.org.uk/sites/default/files/news_articles/documents/Silver%20Chic.Final_.pdf (accessed 16 February 2018).

Damian Utton. *Designing Homes for People with Dementia*. Hawker Publications Ltd, 2006.

Claudia Wood, *The Top of the Ladder*, Demos, 2013, https://www.demos.co.uk/files/TopoftheLadder-web.pdf?1378922386 (accessed 8 February 2018).

Claudia Wood. *Unlocking the Housing Market: Helping first time buyers by helping later life buyers*, Demos, 2017, https://www.demos.co.uk/wp-content/uploads/2017/11/Unlocking-the-Market-Demos-Report.pdf (accessed 16 February 20818).

Women's Royal Voluntary Service (WRVS), *Gold Age Pensioners: Valuing the socio-economic contribution of older people in the UK*, March 2011, https://www.royalvoluntaryservice.org.uk/Uploads/Documents/gold_age_report_2011.pdf (accessed 10 February 2018).

Image credits

p.vi Caroline Teo, New Ground (Case Study 4)
p.viii Tim Crocker, New Ground (Case Study 4)

CHAPTER 1
p.xiv Jacob Birgens / JJW Arkitekter (Faelledgaarden Retirement Home, Copenhagen)
p.4 Crown copyright 2011 (figure redrawn by Levitt Bernstein)
p.7 Mungo Park
p.8 Julia Park
p.10 Levitt Bernstein
p.11 Mungo Park
p.12 Elderly Accommodation Counsel data (figure redrawn by Levitt Bernstein)
p.13 Levitt Bernstein
p.5 Pollard Thomas Edwards / Steven J Arnold
p.16 Tim Crocker
p.17 Pollard Thomas Edwards / Steven J Arnold
p.21 Tristan Poyser

CHAPTER 2
p.26 Pollard Thomas Edwards Co-design session, New Ground (Case Study 4)
p.30 Benedict Luxemoore
p.31 Tim Crocker
p.33 Nicol Thomas
p.34 Care Suite – Levitt Bernstein
p.34 Laura Graesdal Maajen / JJW Arkitekter
p.35 Torben Eskerod / JJW Arkitekter
p.38 Tim Crocker
p.39 Levitt Bernstein
p.41 Richard Partington

p.42 Sarah Wigglesworth Architects
p.43 Ebbsfleet Development Corporation
pp.44–45 (All) Levitt Bernstein
p.46 Tim Crocker
p.50 (Both) Anders Hviid / JJW Arkitekter
p.51 Adam MØrk
p.52 Wimshurst Pelleriti
p.53 Glenn Howells Architects
p.54 De Hogeweyk (Case Study 15)

CHAPTER 3
p.56 Caroline Teo, New Ground (Case Study 4)
p.58 Richard Chivers
p.59 Tim Crocker
p.61 (top) Torben Eskerod / JJW Arkitekter; (bottom) Richard Chivers;
p.62 (top) Caroline Teo; (bottom) De Hogeweyk (case study 15)
p.65 Mie Hampen / The Association of Danish Podiatrists
p.67 Tim Crocker
p.68 Tim Crocker
p.69 Tim Crocker
p.70 Benedict Luxemoore
p.71 Mungo Park
p.72 Tim Crocker

CHAPTER 4
p.74 Torben Eskerod / JJW Arkitekter (Albertshoj Retirement Home, Denmark)
p.76 Rob Rhodes, Renderloft
p.77 Edmund Sumner
pp.78–79 Both Levitt Bernstein
p.80 Tim Crocker

p.81 ornaments (top) Caroline Teo; (bottom) Copenhagen Municipality
pp.82–83 (Three images) Rob Rhodes, Renderloft
p.84 Courtesy of Motionspot
p.85 Tim Crocker
p.87 Architype
p.88 Rob Rhodes, Renderloft
pp.89–90 Both Tim Crocker
p.91 Dean Hawkes
p.92 Levitt Bernstein

CHAPTER 5
p.94 Torben Eskerod / JJW Arkitekter Ørestad Retirement Home, Copenhagen (Case Study 13)
p.97 buddi
p.99 Clare Murray
p.100 Designing with downsizers
p.101 Levitt Bernstein
p.102 The University of Sheffield, DWELL project
p.106 Jo Okpako
p.109 OXOUK
p.110 Priestmann Goode

CHAPTER 6
p.112 Tim Crocker New Ground (Case Study 4)
p.117 Future Facility, illustration Frederic Raetsch
p.117 Yves Behar / Fuseproject

CASE STUDIES
pp.118–119 Phillip Riley (Meadow View, Case Study 14)
pp.120–121 (plan) Evans Vettori Architects and (images) Tristan Poyser

pp.122–123 (plan) Archadia and (images) Charlotte Wood
pp.124–125 (plan) Bell Phillips and (images) Edmund Sumner
pp.126–127 (plan) Pollard Thomas Edwards and Joe Okpako 2 women, Caroline Teo Kitchen and Tim Crocker Balconies
pp.128–129 (plans) Kirsti Sivén & Asko Takala Arkkitehdit Oy / Architects and (images) Asko Takala (left) and Tuomas Uusheimo (right)
pp.130–131 (plan) Proctor and Matthews; (Images) Tim Crocker
pp.132–133 (plans) Levitt Bernstein (images) Tim Crocker
pp.134–135 (plans) DK-Architects (images) Tim Crocker
pp.136–137 (plan) PRP (images) Andy Marshall;
pp.138–139 Mae (for everything apart from the) bottom left of p.139 (which is) Forbes Massie
pp.140–141 (All) Witherford Watson Mann Architects
pp.142–143 (All) Ryder Architecture
pp.144–145 (top) (images) Julia Park (1st two) and (Dining Image) Torben Eskerod / JJW Arkitekter & (and sofa image) Anders Hviid / JJW Arkitekter
pp.146–147 (plan) Glancy Nicholls and (images) Phillip Riley
pp.148–149 (plan) Molenaar & Bol & VanDillen Architects, (yellow kiosk) De Hogeweyk, (images of street view and outdoor sitting areas) Madelaine Sars

Index